Shivah

A Novel from Memory

Shivah

A Novel from Memory
Lisa Solod

JADED IBIS PRESS

Copyright © 2022 by Lisa Solod
First Edition. All Rights Reserved

ISBN: 978-1-938841-72-9

Printed in the USA. No part of this book may be used or reproduced in any manner without written permission from the publisher, except in the case of brief quotations embodied in critical articles or reviews. For information, please email: info@jadedibispress.com. This book is also available in electronic book format.

Solod, Lisa
Shivah / Solod
Cover Design by Crystal J. Hairston

Published by Jaded Ibis Press.
http://www.jadedibispress.com

JADED IBIS PRESS

Praise for *Shivah*

"Solod gives her readers a command performance—one that leaves the reader filled with empathy and sympathy both."
—**Linda Gray Sexton** author of *Searching for Mercy Street: My Journey Back to My Mother, Anne Sexton* and *Half in Love: Surviving the Legacy of Suicide*

"'I didn't know which mother to grieve,' Lisa Solod writes in her closely observed and heartbreaking novel *Shivah*. As her mother sinks deeply into Alzheimer's, Leah must come to terms with a broken relationship that now will never have time to heal. With a journalist's eye and a daughter's heart, Solod puts her character on a quest for the pearl of peace in the dark water of bitterness and loss—a painful journey that will leave readers deeply moved."
—**Jacquelyn Mitchard**, author of *The Deep End of the Ocean*

"*Shivah* is a beautiful, moving meditation on the multiple, complex, and often conflicting layers of grief. Through her narrator's spiraling introspection, Solod asks what it means to lose someone long before you've lost them, to grieve what might have been as well as what was."
—**Ilana Masad**, author of *All My Mother's Lovers*

"The ritual of shivah offers comfort and connection, a way to let mourners know they are not alone in their grief. Lisa Solod's thoughtful, moving novel named for this ritual does the same. Anyone who's dealt with an alcoholic mother, or an emotionally abusive mother, or a mother with dementia or similarly painful and complicated issues, will find comfort and connection in these pages. I found so many echoes of my own complex mother and our tangled relationship in this novel, myself, and am grateful for the sisterhood and insight Lisa Solod provides."

—Gayle Brandeis, author of The Art of Misdiagnosis

To my mother

Shivah: Hebrew for seven. The weeklong period of grief and mourning for the seven closest relations: Father, mother, son, daughter, brother, sister, and spouse. The elements of Shivah (enumerated in the contents below) are all carried out simultaneously throughout the first week of mourning. But grief has its own timetable.

TABLE OF CONTENTS

1. The Heart-Wrenching Pain of Grief and Loss
2. The Ceremony of the Washing of the Hands
3. The Condolence Meal
4. The Telling of Stories
5. The Reciting of the Prayers for the Dead: The Kaddish
6. The Examination of the Souls of Those Still Living
7. The Statements of Comfort for Those Who Remain Behind

Epilogue as Prologue

Every time we enter Mother's hospice room, my daughter Ivy throws herself across her grandmother's body. She is careful to sidle up to Mother slowly and then stretch her long, thin frame against a woman who was also once long and thin but who has shrunk into half of herself. The two of them don't even take up all of the single bed.

It surprises me, this passionate expression of love without fear. Ivy has always been somewhat fearful, delicate, anxious. As she grew older, the world at large shocked her, dismayed her, frightened her. She pushed against it as best she could, and when we entered Mother's room for the first time, it seemed as if everything Ivy had always feared dropped away. She is and will always be pure love and patience.

For more than half of Ivy's life her grandmother has been sick. And for more than a half dozen years Mother hasn't even known who Ivy is, hasn't remembered that she even has a grandchild. Yet Ivy's attachment to Mother is profound: Ivy's memory stops at all the years Mother had held her and played with her. Like Mother, she is okay with forgetting the past few years. Ivy lifts her head up to remind me of the time that she, at six, gave Mother a hairdo which consisted of a dozen tiny clips scattered about her grandmother's Jewish afro. Mother, who didn't love to play at all, allowed Ivy free reign.

Mother's hair has gotten so thin we can see her scalp through it. She is conscious of nothing, not where she is or who is with her on the bed or off. Ivy takes tiny breaks from her vigil. She runs and gets us food, she bends in yoga poses, she speaks to us in hushed tones, and then she is back on the bed with her grandmother as though it will be impossible for Mother to leave this Earth as long as Ivy is connecting her to it. We spend ten days like this, sharing shifts with my sister Erika, but feeling always as if we have never left the room. It feels like a vigil without end and one that began so many years before.

My mother's death, no matter how much expected, is still shocking. She is on her side, completely still, her face turned to the window. Mother's elegant Roman nose, her profile, worthy of an ancient coin, rests against the pillow. The wrinkles that once raddled her cheeks are smoothed as if ironed. She looks ten years younger.

Mother has been practically silent for a few years, save for the intense keening and screaming when the attendants in her nursing home used to bathe or dress her. But this particular silence, the quiet before she leaves forever, is profound: It sucks the air from the room, and we can hear nothing. No cars. No people walking down the hall. No chattering outside our door. Most of us in the room speak quietly in a near-whisper, as if Mother can hear us. And who knows? Perhaps she can. The only ones who speak normally are medical staff: the doctor who pops in to assess "progress" and the nurses who administer Mother's cocktail of pain and antipsychotic meds every four hours—as soon as Mother's legs begin to move restlessly under the covers, a movement that reminds me of her hospitalization four years ago. When she got up from her bed and ran down the hall all those years ago, they strapped her in with restraints. She never walked again.

Ivy whispers things the rest of us can't hear, a rolling litany like davening. My mother's sister, Hannah, and I take turns sitting at Mother's head and watching her breathe. Erika stands at the back of the room for a few minutes after her shift ends. My husband, Paul, looks helplessly on. As a doctor, he knows what is coming. When she breathes her last, he will confirm it and then get the hospice doctor in to confirm it again.

I stroke Mother's head, her cheek, the hand that lays on top of the blanket, and I say, "You can go now." I don't mean it. And I do mean it. But I don't like to say it.

The Heart-Wrenching Pain of Grief and Loss

Accepting the inevitable.
Sh'ma Yis-ra-eil, A-do-nai E-lo-hei-nu, A-do-nai E-chad

1.

My mother had forgotten how to write her name. Several years into her disease she couldn't hold a pen, couldn't remember her name or how to sign a document. There was fear in her eyes when she was asked to put her signature to paper.

Once writing was all she had and all she did. She called herself a writer even if she did most of her work in her head, never put most of it to the page. Even if she wrote the same story over and over, a fictionalized, metaphorical account of her own deep unhappiness. But that writing left her many, many years ago. A few years into her disease, she could not even write who she was in the moment, never mind who she *was*.

I found a journal of Mother's when I was cleaning out her house. In it were her earliest writings: teenaged woes, perhaps typical, but filled with anguish, sadness, inadequacy. She was sixteen years old and like any sixteen-year-old she thought that those moments, those slices of now, were what would shape her forever. The despair of it was heartbreaking: *Will someone ever love me? Will I get into college? Do I really have friends? Am I pretty?*

I felt that way at sixteen, too. The world was too much with me and too large at once. I suspected my daughter did, too, although she was a less angst-ridden teen than I. Her anxieties surfaced later, as she slid unwillingly into her twenties, during those years when all teenagers no longer feel quite like a child and not quite an adult, full of the surety of their maturity and the terror of their insecurity. But reading Mother's anguish it seemed easy to see how her mental illness would manifest later.

Shortly after I found Mother's journal, I burned all of mine in a great bonfire in the firepit out in the yard, freeing ripped pages fistful by fistful, hesitating for only a moment as my past went up in flames. I knew I could not bear it if my daughter found them: They were full of men who had made me happy and made me despair, a litany that categorized how little I knew myself. I no longer recognized that young woman, and I did not wish to introduce her to my child.

Those first few years after the diagnosis and well before she disappeared in everything but body, as Mother began her long and inexorably slow march toward death with me as its chief narrator, I recalled again and again those of her first writings, those self-indulgent, childish diary entries and how they seemed such an easy premonition of Mother's lifelong preoccupation with her *self*. A preoccupation that would cause so many in her family to keep their emotional distance. But no one ever saw these words until I unearthed them, no one read them as a frightening presage to what would make up the entirety of Mother's life. Instead, all we had was her past, present, future selfishness and egotism and how those coexisted with her mental illnesses, making it so very, very hard to love her. Had we known she was damaged from an early age, had we understood how ill she was before she was ill with her final sickness, would we have done things differently? I cannot know.

The last pieces of Mother's writing I saw were hot pink Post-it notes stuck willy-nilly all over her walls, her non-functioning computer, the television, the door out of her room: *Buy mascara. Thank the girls for the flowers. Don't forget to call Hannah.*

Then, all the writing was gone. Mother's name was gone. She could not chronicle her days. She could not write them down in anguish. She could not mark their pain. Mother's days disappeared like dust motes, flying off into the sky. They disappeared like the magician's girl in the magic box, but there was no trick to it. And Mother would never know that she could not remember how to write her name.

2.

Six months after Mother's definitive diagnosis we all began to get an idea what the rest of Mother's life, and the rest of ours, might look like when my younger sister Sara called to tell me a story. She had been to a restaurant with Erika, our youngest sister, our aunt Hannah, and Mother.

"What should I order?" Mother asked Sara.

"What do you *want*?" Sara countered.

"I don't know."

"What do you like?"

"I'm not sure."

"You like salmon, right?" Sara remained patient.

"I like salmon," Mother said.

"Then have the salmon."

"I'll have the salmon," Mother said. But Sara felt Mother said it like she had been forced to eat salmon. Mother was testy and impatient, familiar reactions that were at odds with her sudden helplessness. The waitress was sent away and asked to return. Twice. She stood for the third time at the end of the table. Sara ordered the rack of lamb, Erika said she would have the trout, Mother's sister, Hannah, said she wasn't quite ready yet and the waitress should go on to Mother. The waitress looked at Mother.

"What am I having?" Mother asked the table.

"You're having the salmon," Erika said.

"Oh, is that what you chose for me?"

"No," Sara said. "It is what you *want*."

"I want the salmon," Mother said to the waitress. Then she turned to Erika and said, "You know I won't be able to eat all of it. Will you take it home with you?"

"I'll take it home," Erika said. Erika would not. She would toss it into the garbage.

"Okay then," Hannah said. "I'm ready."

Mother suddenly asked, "Should I have an appetizer?"

"Do you *want* an appetizer?" Hannah asked back.

"I can't eat all that," Mother said.

"Eat what you want," Erika said. "I'll take the rest home."

"Well, in that case . . ." Mother's defiance wandered off.

"We can share an appetizer," Hannah said.

After Mother finished her meal, she sat back, looked at the empty plate and said, "What did I have?"

Two weeks before that lunch, Mother emailed Sara to say she was doing well but that she was sad she did not take a beach vacation that year. Sara passed the email along to me because not three weeks before that email I *had* taken Mother on a beach vacation. A year earlier, before Mother's diagnosis, a month had been reserved. But when it became clear that a month was far too long, I called the woman whose cottage it was and exchanged Mother's four weeks alone for one with me as her caregiver.

Beginning when I was twelve, Mother had taken a month each summer in a house on Cape Cod near her sister Hannah—different houses each time, different villages. My father gave this gift to her when he became successful. When we were young, he would come up for one week a summer: It was mostly Mother, my two sisters, Erika and Sara, and me.

Getting there without my father was hard work. Mother was never a confident driver; her hands clutched tight the wheel of her station wagon while we rolled around in the back, making too much noise, completing the reading of our special comic books in the first hour of the trip, and then begging to stop. She screamed at us, pulled over to the side of the road, told us she was losing her mind. We were no longer shocked by this revelation. She had been crazy for too long.

Two eight-hour days divided by a stop at a cheap motel where we would fight over who did not have to sleep with Mother while she would pour scotch into a glass from the bathroom. And then when we arrived at Hannah's house, Mother would beg for a cocktail, no matter what time it was. The next morning, we would set off to find whichever house she had rented in whichever town called to her, her demeanor growing from agitated to anticipatory as we crossed the bridge from mainland to peninsula.

Mother was different at the Cape, calmer, lazier, smoother. Her drinking slowed, her hands did not shake, and she did not spend hours each day in bed. She walked the length of the beach instead. She fed us fried clams and French fries and ice cream. We were even more ignored than usual. We almost liked her.

When we all left home, Mother went to the Cape alone. Then after Erika moved to a small island called Mashatoc, Mother would rent there instead. Each trip, each year, Mother would devise a new, alternative life for that summer month: She got away from who she was, no matter who she was at the time. She tried to be another woman completely.

But her expectations of the month were always enormous. Mother was like a child whose eyes were bigger than her stomach. She expected transformation, epiphany, catharsis, romance. None of that happened, really, although she wrote in a pseudo diary comprised of unattached papers—that we found floating in a file cabinet decades later—about moments of great discovery that did not seem to last long.

Those weeks at the beach during my youth and beyond were the only time I could remember my mother as anything close to happy.

Before that vacation, the doctors told us that Mother was very healthy. Except for the loss of her mind, of course. Other than that, she was in great shape. Even her liver, an organ that by all rights should have been a puddle of cellular mutation, was sound. We were told Mother would live a long time yet. To me that sounded not like a blessing but like a curse. The kind of curse the bad fairy put on Sleeping Beauty at her birth; the kind of curse it would take a lifetime to undo. A lifetime that was already over.

"Don't agonize over what your mother recalls or doesn't," Dr. Godwin told us when he first explained what Mother had. He cautioned us that taking her out of a safe space might provoke anxiety but that we should ignore that and take her out as often as we could. Her memory of the anxiety would recede as quickly as the memory of the trip or the event. Dr. Godwin said, "Take her out for *you*." He told us that somewhere inside, deep inside but inaccessible, all the experiences Mother had were trapped—there but trapped in a locked box, the combination long forgotten. Even if there was no way to rekey the lock, Dr. Godwin said everything was still in there. I didn't believe him. He was just guessing, like everyone else. No one knew for sure. Not then, certainly. Despite patients deep in the throes of Alzheimer's who suddenly sing along to an old song from their youth, we have no idea *what* is still stored or *where* it is stored. We don't know if it is still really there or why some things reappear and others don't. Why some things last and others disappear for good.

And so, I felt the absolute necessity of giving her some more time by the sea even if, in this case, Mother would finally be that whole other person she had tried to conjure for most of her life.

SHIVAH

The island where Mother rented a house for years was nearly as small as her tiny, borrowed house, holding perhaps fifty families year-round and swelling to several hundred each summer. It was no more than two miles long and a mile wide, much of it a nature preserve. You reached it via ferry or private boat. It was lonely and lush and perfect and more than a little crazy, as the few natives illustrated. My sister Erika lived on the island, had for years since she married a man who had a house there. Erika was sure Mother had given up the Cape and chosen the island just to spite her.

Mother's relationship with her three daughters was fraught and debilitating, but in a different way for each of us. I never thought Mother rented in Erika's backyard to deliberately annoy her. She needed her. Erika was the most placid of us three. She hated confrontation. It seemed obvious that as Mother aged, she needed a touchstone, someone just up the hill she could rely on during her solitary time at the sea. She didn't mean to be intrusive and annoying; she just was. It was her nature.

Although Erika played the dutiful daughter each summer, she would also call me five or six times during that time, to regale me with some story or another of how Mother had misbehaved. Over the years Mother's behavior grew increasingly bizarre and belligerent, but we all put it down to her drinking, her mental instability, her age. To the disappointments accrued over an entire life. None of us wanted to parse

Mother's unhappiness any further than we had to.

That first week with Mother was a nearly unbearable. I had a front row seat to the way she had changed seemingly overnight. The glamorous, self-absorbed, brash and difficult woman I had known all my life had become a timorous, fragile, vague woman I hardly recognized. I felt a little nuts for volunteering to take her away in the first place.

As soon as the official diagnosis had been pronounced, it was as if Mother fell headfirst into it. As if, with all the strength she could muster, she had just been barely holding herself back from jumping into an abyss. But now she had permission to hurl herself over the edge, to fly, plunge, rocket to the bottom. Or what seemed like the bottom. How were we to know that bottom was still so very, very far away? That Mother would float, airborne, hands out, for years and years until finally, gently yet excruciatingly, she would land in a puddle at the bottom of the cliff: The hospice room where she died.

But her acceptance of the end of one life and the beginning of another so much narrower and uglier was not a suicide gesture. I had expected that, frankly, expected her to give up on life all at once, take herself out as soon as she realized her future was gone. Mother had, after all, spent a good part of her life threatening to kill herself. Warning those around her that she was just *this close* to the edge. *If you tell me something, anything, that I'm responsible for, I will just slit my wrists and be gone with it*, she threatened more than once, whenever any of us children tried to bring up a difficult subject. An idle threat, apparently. Mother wanted to live. She didn't seem to much care how.

Her end would not be sudden or swift. It would be a slow, dipping, swirling descent into the emptiness of the rest of her nonexistent future. Subterfuge was gone—we all knew what was happening—and there was no way to get through the next so many years without willingly, consciously, accepting it as she had. It was clearly a lot easier for her.

Most of that week Mother and I sat silently on the sand and quietly watched the water. But one night we visited a couple who had been Mother's friends during her decades on the island. I saw the sympathy and sadness in their eyes. They greeted her with animation and enthusiasm, but when they hugged her, they looked sadly over her shoulder at me and mouthed, I'm sorry.

People knew. We didn't have to tell anyone, they just knew—the woman who ran the breakfast place, the woman who ran the grocery store, the couple who had been coming to the island for a half century, the friends of my sister who had been, in the past, gracious and forgiving of Mother and her behaviors. They all hugged her, some of them with tears in their eyes, but they were uncomfortable; few of them invited us in. If they had a moment alone with me, they would tell me quickly how awful it was that something like this had to happen to such a vibrant woman. I didn't blame them for their lack of invitations. Being with Mother was extraordinarily hard work.

    Twice Mother and I drove up the long, steep hill to Erika's house for dinner. A mere two months after she was pronounced sick, Mother's appetite was still pretty good. She hadn't yet taken to just pushing food around on her plate. That would come in year three or four and then last forever. But Mother had never been much of an eater, anyway; she spent her life dieting, giving herself enemas for weight control, punishing her body with alcohol instead of food. That wouldn't change for a while either.

    The first evening at Erika's, Mother got very angry when my sister told her that she had to wait until dinner for a glass of wine. I will always remember that Mother never liked being refused anything; that particular vestige of her personality persisted longer than any other. Her haughty annoyance at being thwarted was part and parcel of her. And Mother was a drunk, had been for a good portion of her life. So anything surrounding alcohol was going to be a battle.

    I stayed out of the fray that particular night because I didn't have the heart to tell Erika that I was letting Mother drink all she wanted down at our little cottage, that I had stocked it liberally with Mother's particular brand of cheap, oversized bottles of chardonnay. I didn't have the strength to tell my sister that I wasn't going to spend a week in a tiny fairy cottage on a small island in the middle of the ocean with a woman who had just been given a death sentence *without* the special lubrication Mother required. She needed wine to get through the day. I needed Mother to get through the day.

Despite the forced drying out that had illuminated Mother's real disease, I was not going to deny her. She might have been losing her mind, but she had reminded me several times to buy wine when we loaded up at the supermarket on the mainland before we got on the ferry. I bought half a case under her direct supervision. It was my insurance policy.

During our week at the cottage, the weather was perfect, always an iffy proposition for a New England island town. Perhaps God was being kind. Perhaps He felt sorry for her, for us, that things had turned out like this. Perhaps He understood happiness better than I always imagined. Mother and I took long beach walks, well, long for a woman who in the past had been used to walking miles, head up, back straight, her long legs traversing the sand like a warrior. In other words, we walked for minutes. I placed a hand on Mother's elbow when she would let me, steadying her over the rocks, the bumps in the sand; as her memory untethered, she assumed an unsteadiness on her feet that would come and go. (She would get her legs back a couple of years later, how we never knew, and for most of the following decade, she never used the walker that sat like a sentinel in the corner of the many rooms she occupied. Until at last, her companion was a wheelchair.) But that first summer she was so fragile and so unstable in every way.

Most of the specifics of that first summer became hazy with time. With Mother's memory loss came my own selective memory: I have edited out the worst of it, kept the best, put some other memories in a box to examine later. (I think anyone caring for someone with dementia has to do this.) There was a daily intensity of simply moving about the tiny cottage space, of cooking for Mother, of keeping her safe, of watching her as I would a toddler. It was enervating. I had cared for a sick child more than once, of course, but caring for Mother was a different story. There were so many moving parts. And so new to her newness, my hackles were still up; I felt like my pugilistic stance, honed over half a century, was unlikely to be easily shrugged out of. If we didn't fight, what did we have?

But I do remember that I almost completely exhausted myself that week. It wasn't just the cooking and washing up and the caretaking. That was easy. It was having the same conversation more than a dozen times a day in an endless loop: small conversations about almost nothing or large conversations about almost nothing. I woke each morning nearly drowning in the anticipation of a day that would be the same as each before. It was my first extended amount of time with her since she had been diagnosed, and I wasn't prepared for the repetition of it. I hadn't accounted for all my unspent anger, for my hope that things could change, for the desire for a perfectly loving relationship. I had not yet given up my desire to be recognized. To be seen by Mother.

When I was ill as a young child, Mother would bring me ginger ale and crackers and let me watch old movies while lying on her huge king-sized bed in the room with the black and gold flecked wallpaper that made it seem as though I, too, was on a Hollywood set. Every frame of *Kings Row* and the image Ronald Regan shouting, "Where's the rest of me?" stuck with me through the years.

I think I always knew she loved me even though she never said it. But I also understood it was a toxic love, a dangerous affection for a child who needed her ministrations. And once I outgrew most of my illnesses, she didn't know how to care for me. So she didn't.

Instead we always circled around meaning. Around and around anything of importance. Conversations always turned into explosions. Each innocent comment was loaded with trace evidence, like the body of a murder victim. If she asked me if something I was wearing or a bag I was carrying was new, there was an implicit judgement in the question: I was being extravagant in a way she would not allow herself to be.

When I was a child, she would doubt my word in one breath, and in the next, she would defend me from others. She was my bully. She was my savior. When I was a young adult, we fought like cats and dogs over taking the metro when it was hot and crowded—over nothing. I was still storing up my emotional reserves and had not yet learned how to ignore her when she started on. As an adult, I started hanging up the phone, and in my forties, after days and days of criticism about the way I raised my daughter and the cleanliness of my house, I banished her from my home for two years. I brought Ivy to see her at the cottage, but we stayed with Hannah, not with Mother. Eventually, as always, I let her back into my life, though nothing had changed. I think I was always too weary to keep up the fight.

But there was also the time I found her drunk and weeping. I put my arms around her. I listened to her tell me of an affair with a man she had loved for decades who ultimately rejected her. I recalled a New Year's Eve when a boy I cared for rejected me and she held my head as I vomited vodka. Our whole life we did the same dance. We had done it nearly fifty years.

With her illness the dance would change, but it was still recognizable, for a while. But clearly it was no longer a fair fight. She was operating under a severe handicap, and so I discovered a more gentle side of myself until the dance stopped.

That first summer, Mother and I adopted a new language. At the time, I did not understand that it would become our only language. Clarity was gone. Memory was gone. Old hurts were buried beneath layers and layers of tangled plaque. She would ask how I was, and I needed to be specific or she would ask me again. If I was feeling at all energetic and creative, I might add details that were meaningless but which she hung on to. I regaled her with my daughter Ivy's antics, the same ones, different ones. I told her the news, parsing a litany of the daily events of the world. Mother would nod as though she understood me and then ask me the same questions again and again, each time like they were new. I had no experience with this. I had experience with Mother's cruelty, her anger, her assumptions about my life, my work, my family. That first summer I did not realize that all the exhausting effort I put into listening to those same questions and answering them again and again, over and over, would frame the relationship I would have with Mother for the rest of her life. I never imagined how much worse it could get.

I stood at the sink and looked out the large plate glass window. I watched Mother sitting in a plastic chair on the grass in front of the house. She was completely still. Nearly immobile. I thought about how all her life she had had two ways of being: as wild as a whirling dervish and as immobile and quiet as a corpse. I never knew which woman I would find each day.

Many times the woman who handed me a cereal box for breakfast was not the same woman who picked me up from school. She would cheerfully cook my sisters and me eggs and then be in her bed in the dark at the end of the afternoon. Most of my life I tried so hard to say the thing that would get her eyes to light up, to do the thing that would please her. I wanted very much for her to come out of the dark bedroom and be with me.

In that moment, sitting outside, Mother was as still as I had ever seen her. She gazed out at the water with a supremely content expression on her face: The lines of age and illness and worry smoothed away by a tiny, precious moment of what could only be called bliss. She looked normal.

She looked happy. She looked like her old self. Or perhaps more accurately, she looked like her old self when she was happy and things were going well, which hadn't been often. Or often enough for either of us. With little effort, even with the holes in my own memory I could, if I tried, probably remember every single one of the moments of Mother's limited bliss. The look on her face as she saw the ocean for the first time each summer. The smile she gave the audience after one of her brilliant community theater performances, the pleasure at a meal that my father praised. The times she cheered me on as I pushed through my asthma to win a swimming meet. It wasn't that she hadn't been there for us or that she hadn't been happy sometimes, it was that we never knew which Mother would greet us week to week, day to day, hour to hour. And we had no language to even describe our confusion, a confusion that we saw for too long as just the way things were.

In that moment, on her face was simple and pure and uncomplicated joy. Mother was a child who had been given a fabulous piece of candy, and she was staring at it with astonishment, delight. Children do not realize that as soon as that candy, that moment, dissolves, the memory of it is gone, too. In her case, Mother was lucky to no longer have memories of either happiness or unhappiness: Each emotion existed only for a small, fleeting nanosecond. She could hold on to neither pleasure nor pain.

In a few years I would watch an entertainer come into the locked memory unit where she resided. He set up his microphone and began to sing old show tunes. Mother looked at him askance; he was terrible. I think she understood that. But despite herself, she sang along. She remembered so many of the words. Those songs had far more words than any of our recent conversations.

Despite the doctor's initial "orders" that we not dwell on the loss of Mother's memory, it took me many years to become completely comfortable with the fact that my mother's happiness in any current moment had nothing to do with what was actually happening and nothing to do with what she would or would not remember later. And nothing to do with me.

In the last year before she fell ill and went into the hospital and then into a nursing home for the rest of her life, I wanted to take her to the beach, to Narragansett, to the beach close to where her mother and father had taken my sisters and me as children, to my grandparents' tiny trailer that sat on the large, round rocks that were unlike any beach I have seen since. I knew the trailer was long gone and I wouldn't be able to find that particular beach, but I was determined to take her to the ocean one last time. She said she didn't want to go. I told her we were going anyway. She became almost pliant. I helped her into the car.

It was a stunning New England day, sunny but not too warm, and as we walked along the path by the ocean, it seemed absolutely worth it to get her out of her space and somewhere that used to make her happy. But after ten minutes, she sat down on the rock wall that spanned the sea and said, "I'm tired. Can we go?" and I took her arm and carefully guided her back to the car, and we began the forty-five-minute drive home. I made a stop for lunch, and we split a Reuben. There was a moment of normalcy to it. Still, I felt awful. I had pushed her out of her safe space once again—I was always doing that, it seemed. The day had been a failure. But when we returned and I punched in the numbers to the door of the locked ward, she turned to me and said, "Thank you for the beautiful day."

    I learned that my efforts were truly meaningless except that they made it easier to live with myself. I have since learned to be okay with the fact that the moment, the effort in *making* the moment, is enough. It has to be enough. Mother's tiny frissons of pure happiness were a good thing, even if everything around them turned to shit. Mother could live only in the smallest moment and that had to be enough. It had to be enough. For her. And for me. Even then, nearly a decade after she was diagnosed. But most times when I left her, until the absolute end, I still sat and wept in my car.

3.

According to my mother's sister, Hannah, when the doctors first told Mother about the Alzheimer's, Mother said, "Shit, shit, shit. I knew it." Then she burst into tears. Hannah wept along with her. Then Hannah called my sisters and me. It was suddenly, stupidly clear to all of us that the alcohol abuse had masked the real deterioration going on inside Mother's brain. The deterioration that seemed to go round and round and never end. It had been put down by all of us as merely the effects of too many glasses of wine at the end of the day. It was something far more sinister. We had to confront our laziness, our indifference. The collective desire not to know.

When mother left her marriage to my father, she managed. She worked a job. She moved house twice. She bought a tiny home in the loveliest Providence neighborhood. She had new friends. And then she retired. Shit kept hitting the fan.

She didn't have enough to do with her time. Her drinking intensified. She became belligerent about the amount and kind of wine in all of our refrigerators. She drank coffee until noon, black, no sugar, and then began polishing off a large bottle of cheap chardonnay until she fell asleep.

When I continued to posit that Mother's alcohol abuse had gotten worse and worse and she was no longer what was gently called "a functional drunk," I was met with resistance. From everyone in the family. It wasn't seen as a big enough deal, alcoholism. (Jews didn't have drinking problems, my bubbe had always insisted, even though she'd had to fetch her no-good father from a tavern or bar most of the days of her childhood.) "But she just drinks wine," was said. But I could absolutely remember Mother holding a glass of iced tea, something she never liked, never drank in public, carrying it around the house for the entire day. I could see her sitting on the patio that she turned into a screened porch, rocking back and forth in a hanging basket chair, sipping a never-ending glass. She had been a vodka drinker, hiding it in plain sight. Her switch to wine after the separation and divorce was a way to deceive herself that she wasn't reliant on booze. She wanted us to buy into the lie, too.

So all the time we dithered and dissembled and excused Mother's drinking, Mother's mind had literally been shrinking inside her skull, the fleshy matter peeling away from the bone. Memories disappearing like soap bubbles. There. There. Gone. No doubt now as to the cause of her inability to cope even less well than she did in the past. She was really sick, sick with something physical, something no one could pretend wasn't serious. It was so serious.

Whatever excuses we heard when we were old enough to hear them, excuses made for Mother, *by* us, *to* us, *for* us, about her lifelong inability to cope—a lack of choices for her generation, stress, too many children too fast, drink, mental illness—none of those mattered any longer. As soon as the word *Alzheimer's* was pronounced, Mother pretty much gave up, gave in, waved the white flag on even trying to remember. The diagnosis of what she must have suspected, of what we had remained blind to, allowed her to dissolve herself completely. But she did not give up her alcohol.

She would occasionally struggle against the way the illness limited her—when she could wrap herself around even the concept that she had Alzheimer's at all—but Mother never ever mentioned the word in connection with herself. It was a word that did not exist. Her small flashes of anger and then confusion about what she was angry about to begin with were so soft, so temporary that they seemed almost harmless. To me anyway. They bounced off my hardened flesh like insects. Where once she had been so formidable an opponent that we had only to poke her gently once before we were furiously bitten, now she was a defeated champion, her fists too weak to do real damage any longer. Toothless.

That very first year when she just let go, Dr. Godwin told my sisters and me to be okay with it all. At first, he counseled patience. But as she moved from assisted living to the locked ward, he grew impatient; his directives were less positive, less informative, less helpful. He stopped promptly answering our calls. He didn't like that Mother still drank and he urged us to get her to stop. He said the drinking interfered with her medications. He referred us to neurologists, geriatric psychiatrists. She was taken off some meds and put on others.

I was sitting in Budapest in a café when I got a call that Mother's agitation was such that she had begun saving and flinging her own feces, attacking the nurses with her fists, yelling at staff. It was dark, ten p.m., and I was listening to a violinist and drinking pálinka and six hours earlier in time Mother was melting down. I wept for a good half hour and then gathered my breath and phoned Hannah and asked her to call Erika.

Mother was put on an antipsychotic. It calmed her down, but it further deadened her. It was hard to tell what was making her worse, the course of the disease or the medication. I asked the doctor to cut back the dose a little.

I thought I was new to the disease; I thought it was something I hadn't really heard of, so I read voraciously each challenging article or theory that was published. But I only *thought* I was a novice. When I looked back at the life of my bubbe for the last dozen years of it, I saw the pattern. I saw the heredity. That is when I began to get frightened. I began to put my own affairs in order, plan my own exit.

I read an article about a woman who had been diagnosed, at sixty, with early-onset Alzheimer's. She decided to end her life when she thought things were really slipping. She set everything up: A good-bye party with her family and friends and then she planned to slip away into the bedroom with her husband where she would take enough pills to kill herself. When I told my husband, Paul, about this, he told me there would have to be alcohol with the pills in order to make sure it killed me, so I rethought the plan. Legal or not, there had to be a way to end life before you became an object of pity. Before you disappeared.

And so, for the first few years of Mother's illness I was consumed by my own death. I sat Ivy down and explained to her what I could and could not do if I were diagnosed. What I would and would not do when I found out. Because how could I live with people watching me vanish? There was no way. Of course, Ivy did not wish to talk of my death or me losing my memory, or any of it. No one really does. But I made her talk about it as Mother had never made us. I forced her to listen to me. I was nearly brutal.

I answered that email Mother had sent to Sara. In it I said simply: I took you to the beach, Mother. I took you to the beach and we had a wonderful time.

I sent the same email after the same complaint after our second and last summer at the cottage. There were to be no more weeks at the beach in her fairy house after that.

And very soon into that second year Mother forgot how to use a computer.

4.

As the first months passed and Mother's body began to follow her mind, as her body shrank and her bones looked as if they, too, were beginning to disappear inside her flesh, she looked almost as if she were molting, trying to shed that outer shell that had fooled everyone into thinking she was another kind of animal indeed. A well woman. A woman in control of her life. Mother had always appeared so tall to me, to all of us, stately even, but the truth was that she never had more than a couple of inches on my sisters and me; she just had major presence. But with alarming speed she seemed to grow ever shorter, tinier, more frail. Her back was suddenly slightly hunched, her hair thinned, her high-cheek-boned face crisscrossed with new wrinkles. She was disintegrating.

This was not Mother's first vanishing act. When I was six, she somehow made it from Tennessee to Provincetown alone. Disappearing from the house, materializing in another place, like Houdini's elephant. Once there in Provincetown, the story went, she apparently lay for hours, unobserved, on the coarse Cape Cod sand, close to the water's edge, dressed in one of her costumes: a diaphanous blouse and long, gauzy skirt of marine blue and green. A policeman finally spotted her and asked what she was doing, to which Mother replied that she was a mermaid stranded on shore. Floundering. Gaining purchase. The cop called Father and he flew up and got her. This was all told to us secondhand so many years later. The truth of it eluded us. Who knew who did or said what? Not us.

When she came home Mother rested a lot.

The second time she dematerialized, she was not discovered for days. Father lied and told my sisters and me that Mother was taking a little vacation. It didn't bother us too much as Mother was usually emotionally unavailable even when she was around. She was locked inside herself, even if she was in the same room as we were. No one, again, had any idea where she went. She returned almost two weeks later with no explanation. At least for us. For a while she even acted fairly normal. Until the morning Erika threw a shoe across the kitchen and it landed in Sara's Rice Krispies. Mother broke down weeping. My sisters and I fled to our bedrooms.

Yet, thinking back upon her many disappearances, she had been escaping right in front of our eyes for years. She was an actress in our small but powerful community theater and in the juicy roles she garnered, she metamorphosized: Kate in the *The Taming of the Shrew* and Eleanor of Aquitaine in *The Lion in Winter* and Martha in *Who's Afraid of*

SHIVAH

Virginia Woolf. She assumed these identities with such ease and presence it was like she had these personas up her sleeve the whole time. Watching her, even I could easily forget she was my mother.

5.

One night, in the middle of the first year of Mother's diagnosis, I sat at the bar at my sister Sara's restaurant, sipping a glass of wine and commiserating. We were all still slightly shell-shocked by the ordeal of hearing the diagnosis, cleaning out Mother's house, selling it, and moving her into *Menuchat Lev,* a relatively new and elegant assisted living facility that my uncle had connections to. We were still stuck in the simple confusion of how to react to the complete helplessness of the woman who had so dominated our lives for more than forty years.

"Don't let me have more than one glass," I said, acknowledging, as did we all, the fear that Mother's alcoholism could be in our blood. So much of the time each of us fought against our heredity, not knowing for sure what was bred in the bone and what wasn't. We had worried about being drunks, being crazy. Now we had to worry about losing our *selves.*

Sara's wide-mouthed smile sent her sharp cheekbones

nearly up to her eyes. Her long, dark hair was in its standard braid, hanging down to her waist. She brushed some tendrils off her forehead with the back of her hand, the front marred by the juice from the raw chicken breasts she was cutting off the bone, her arm marked by a row of scars—burn slashes from when she had carelessly reached into a hot oven.

"Don't worry. I'll be the first to let you know when you become a drunk," she said.

"I'm sure you will," I laughed.

"I wish I could really love her, especially now, but I can't. All I feel is sorry for her," Sara suddenly said.

"I feel sorry for her, too," I said. And I did. But I also put paid to Sara's statement. The longer I lived the more I understood that my love for my immediate family would almost always win, no matter how badly I had been treated. My need for a family was so strong that it said something problematic about me, I knew that. I was so dysfunctional that despite the ways my mother emotionally abused me over the years, I still had deep, powerful love for the troubled, angry, sad woman who had tried to raise us and mostly failed. And it ran so deep. I tried to both explain and justify it but all those years of wishing for the kind of unequivocal love that I had for Ivy actually wound up making her easier to love once her damaged brain wouldn't let her love me back.

Over the past two decades, as I had tried to extricate myself from her fury and her pain, her blame and her misery, I had continued to love her, even as she made herself more and more unlovable. But as much as we might have suffered from Mother's toxicity, we all reacted in different ways, with different tolerances. Even before she got so sick, I had long ago given up trying to get something from her. But I did think that both Sara and Erika still expected something of her, although I had no idea what.

"You know, it's funny," I said, looking hard at Sara, willing her to look me in the eyes. "When mother used to come visit me, she would throw hand grenades into the room at any opportunity. It took me a long time to learn not to fire back, not to lob a grenade at her. She will say I did, naturally—I am sure she told her shrink what an ungrateful harridan her oldest daughter was—but whatever I threw back was not nearly the caliber of what had been tossed at me. Small-bore bullets against an AK-47. I never could actually surrender, but I did eventually learn that if I just refused the battle, if I stopped tossing anything into the mix, even a pocketknife or a slingshot, she would stop.

"People can't keep throwing stuff at a person who doesn't fight back," I said. Eventually, I learned that. Mother might have continued to throw for a while but without the power of me accepting them and tossing my own weapons into the mix, the grenades would just fizzle out rather than explode.

"It took me a very long time to get to that place. You know that." But I could tell Sara wasn't really listening. She couldn't engage in an unemotional accounting of either of our parents. Her anger was always too close to the surface. Once when someone who knew the three of us said, "You're all so interesting. Your parents did a good job of raising you," Sara, through clenched teeth, hissed, "We raised ourselves."

Nonetheless I persisted in trying to work on my feelings about what was happening with Mother and us. And the guilt, especially the guilt. Even though Mother could no longer lob the huge, damaging grenades that blew up my life, she did toss a little stink bomb here and there. One visit, she would complain about how unhappy she was at *Menuchat Lev*, about how we sold her house out from under her, about how everyone else at the residence was old and sick and boring. But there was no real venom in her words: The snake had been defanged. On another visit, Mother might turn around and thank me for getting us to the safety of her current home, but the gratitude in those words was as limp as her fury used to be. She was a smoothed, tamped down, nearly dull version of herself and yet I still felt bad about selling her house from under and allowing both Mother and me to give into the stasis of her disease.

I sighed, racked with responsibility that Sara did not seem to feel. "I mean, think about it: How long did she live in her house, afraid to go out, to drive, unable to even remember how to cook a meal, or shop for groceries? And how long did we ignore the slow deterioration of her mind, thinking she was just drunk? Again. And again."

No one could bully me as well as I could bully myself.

"All those late-night conversations I put down to her having gone over her quota of wine. But she was lost and scared. We knew it but we didn't. Maybe. None of us wanted to know that."

"I know," Sara said. "But what did we really do? What did we do but take away everything familiar? Force her into a . . . a home, a residence, whatever it is."

"That's a lot," I said, knowing that Sara had no hand in most of it. Erika and I had done the work. But I knew, too, none of us ever had a real choice. Although I had half-heartedly floated the idea of Mother coming south to live near Sara and me so we could split the care of her, I knew it wasn't a sincere offer because I knew that Sara's guilt wasn't as large as mine. She hadn't inherited that gene.

"We had no choice, Sara," I said. When the truth hit us in the face, we didn't flinch. We didn't curl up into ourselves. We acted, we found a safe place because there had been no other real choice. Any offer for her to live with us would have been a lie. And she made it clear she wanted to stay in New England where she had friends. Those friends would fall away from her in the next few years, daunted by Mother's deteriorating condition. Yet we made the best decision we could.

Sara put down her knife. "I'm really not sure how much longer I can do this," she said. She took a small sip from her own glass of wine. People would be coming into the restaurant in an hour or so for dinner. She looked harried.

"The restaurant?"

"Everything. I'm so tired." I reached over and touched Sara's scarred arm. It occurred to me that putting one's arm into a fire could be a choice, too.

"We can only do what we can do," I said. "We visit, we try. And then we have to let go." I sensed that Sara was already gone in some ways. She avoided cleaning out Mother's house, avoided the move into assisted living. She would use her work as a reason to visit less and less. Her tolerance for fire had obviously much diminished over time.

"Mother still writes me these long emails. She calls me and tells me how much she hates that place," Sara said. "Should we just have left her in her home?"

"You know full well that was impossible. Those narrow wooden stairs to the second floor, the concrete stairs to the basement. The tiny, hot bedrooms. Where would we have put a carer? She couldn't be alone."

"I know," Sara said, already tired of the conversation. "For years and years, I kept waiting for that call in the middle of the night, the call to tell me she had fallen down the stairs or she'd had a car accident. Sometimes I would wake up and think: That's it, she's gone. And now, in a way, she *is* gone. But she's still around. And in and out of herself. Sometimes when she calls, she sounds just like she always did . . ."

"And that pushes a whole other set of buttons," I said. "I know."

"Yes, that pushes a whole other set of buttons indeed."

"But soon," I said, "the emails will stop, the phone calls will end. Already she forgets that she talked to me yesterday and she calls the next day and I tell her the same news and stories all over again.

"Look, Sara. I got through a week at the beach alone

with her and we've all kept up a semblance of order. This is just how it's going to be for the foreseeable future."

I knew that Erika saw her almost every week. Hannah had her over for any possible event. Old friends stopped by. Even though Mother always said that no one came, when I looked at her calendar, it was filled with things she'd done. She complained nothing happened but that was always her way. That last year at her house, at the least, she never even went out. She hardly ate; all she did was drink. The house was a mess. It looked okay when you first went in, but, oh the closets, the spare rooms, the basement were all stuffed to overflowing, like she was hiding the chaos from us. It was so obvious that we could never have left her there. Still, I knew Sara was angry because she felt that Mother made so little effort with us. That we were going way beyond duty. Perhaps. But I didn't believe that. I felt strongly that we had the old-fashioned Biblical imperative.

I sat back and slowly sipped my wine. We had been blind, willfully so. We had ignored the signs until they became so obvious that we could not deny their significance. The empty pantry, the out-of-date food in the refrigerator, the unpaid bills. When her hairdresser called Hannah and told her Mother had missed the past three appointments, it shocked us. We would later learn she had forgotten how to get to his salon. Our punishment, so to speak, was to spend the next however many years making up for that.

I told Sara there was a Yiddish proverb that went, "When a father gives to his son, both laugh. When a son gives to his father, both cry."

"And?"

"This is the natural order of things, to be in the kind of situation we are; the fact that *we* take care of *her*. It's bound to make us feel sad and helpless. It's inherent in the nature of it."

Sara looked at me and I shrugged. "Man plans; God laughs." I lifted my shoulders again. I asked Sara if she thought that our past with Mother made it easier or harder to cope with Mother like this. I wondered if it would have made a difference if we had one of those storybook loving relationships with Mother. Would we be in tears each time we saw her? Would her fading from view affect us in a different way? Would the devastation be greater?

"Maybe," Sara said. "I don't know. I can't know that. All I know is that I feel pretty much about her as I always did. Indifferent if I can manage it, angry when I am caught unawares, and constantly curious as to how she came to be like she came to be. And then I wonder, was she ever happy with herself, with her life? Can she, will she, be happy now?"

I have long wondered if happiness or its opposite isn't hard-wired in the brain. There are those of us who can manage it and those who cannot, no matter the circumstances. I once heard a scientist talk about how we have a sort of super sense, a deep intuitiveness that is, well, genetic, I guess. It's there in the brain from the get-go. It's why we believe things that are unbelievable, unverifiable. Like God.

But what if happiness *is* hardwired? I mean we all know that people have a disposition toward mental illness, alcoholism, depression, and any number of other diseases and syndromes. There is even, apparently, a shyness gene, and I once read, with fascination, an article claiming that resiliency is something that is located deep within the brain. I am quite frankly intrigued by my own resilience. I have often felt stronger the more crap that was thrown at me. So if the ability of people to withstand trauma when others cannot is in our heads from birth, why not the capacity for happiness?

When I brought this up to Sara some years ago she said: "But there are so many different levels of happiness. No one's is the same. No country's or society's is the same. You've seen the studies on contentment. It's grounded in some realities and something very... fuzzy. Maybe those belief systems you talk about.

"And maybe the idea of happiness at all is overrated. Look at art. Does it come from happy people? It does not. It comes from trauma and melancholy and displacement and even mental illness. It comes from people who are trying to work out their own unhappiness on the page or the canvas or the screen."

"Yes," I argued, "but day to day, can one choose to see what is good and positive, rather than what is dark and despairing, or have we no choice in the matter? Is happiness something that can't be imagined. Like pain? You can imagine what happiness *might* be like, how it *might* feel, because you can conjure up the idea of pain but not the actual feeling."

Maybe happiness is not a choice at all. Why else would Mother have chosen not to be happy and instead opted to be so unhappy? It had taken us a long time to realize our mother had a mental illness. Children don't understand shades of gray: They see behaviors and how those behaviors affect them. As teens we are even more solipsistic. When I was in my early twenties and Mother had her nervous breakdown, I started to understand a little better. But the existence of something as complex as bipolar disease was not in our vernacular. She was *just* depressed, right? She *just* needed a break. Her children had flown the nest, her marriage was in shambles. She *just* needed a breather, time to figure out who she was without all the trappings of the "hoods": wife/mother/housewife. But she could never get around the fact of her mental illness; she couldn't even acknowledge it.

Why did she live in denial and force us live with a mother who was so frenetic one day, so enervated the next? And none of us knew the truth for so long. We didn't know what mental illness was. We always thought, like most children, that our existence was normal, or at least on the outskirts of normal. It didn't occur to us until later in life that there was something explicable about the way that, even when she was manic or energetic, she wasn't happy. And no matter what, she relished when we came to her with bad news. She seemed to enjoy a crisis. I didn't understand for too long that it made her feel needed. But we learned to lie and tell her everything was fine because that was the only way to distance ourselves emotionally, even after we had distanced ourselves physically

Sara thought Erika and I did a better job managing our relationships with Mother than she did. But I wasn't so sure. The three of us each had our ways of coping, of dissembling. Mother and I had long had a dance. We each knew our steps and who was leading at any given time. Our roles were acceptable to us even as we hated them. Or at least I hated mine. I was the lousy, ungrateful daughter and Mother was the uncaring, emotionally needy, selfish mom. Well into young adulthood I tried to change who Mother was or pretend she was something other than what I knew to be true. I was in denial, big time, as was Mother. But we still fell into our dance. The rabbis tell us that denial is the symptom of an overblown ego. We were both guilty.

I told Sara that for forever, Mother wanted me to be someone else, although I have no idea who, nor do I think she did, either. I think both she and I continued to carry around a fantasy of the perfect mother-daughter relationship. Maybe because I was her first. Sara got to be the tormented, misunderstood middle child and Erika got to be the sweet, placid baby.

Being the baby left Erika all kinds of room for bad behavior that Mother wouldn't have tolerated in me, for instance. She was allowed freedoms which were denied to me and Sara, independence that we had craved. Her curfew was nonexistent; she had her own car; she wasn't required to sit and make conversation at the dinner table over an evening. It could have been merely because by the time Erika was in the house alone with Mother and Father, they were exhausted. But, too, she didn't have two sisters to fight with. So it was hard for us to imagine her life as it seemed so at odds with our own, or at least our memory of it. And Mother was already slowly falling apart. We understood that. Later.

Although it would take me years to acknowledge it, my whole life shifted in a single moment. That night, that shift, made it possible for me, fifteen years later, to let go, with a huge whoosh, all the anger and sorrow I had felt for myself and for Mother. The past left my body all at once and I was a clean slate who would care for my mother for the rest of her life. Guilt begets responsibility, if it's done right, I guess. My penance for cutting out my mother's heart was to give her mine.

    It started when I when I found myself frustrated by a fussy baby in a house that wasn't my own, that I didn't feel safe in. I became unmoored. I was without my husband, Ben, as I had been up visiting my mother in Providence. My father had invited us all, Erika, Sara, and me, to his house on the island, despite the fact that he hadn't yet furnished it. Mother invited herself to the island for a few days and my father, who could never refuse her in the small things, said all right. It was night; it was dark; I had no idea where any of us would sleep; my parents were in a room together for the first time since my wedding: All ingredients for a war. And I threw the first punch.

Now that I had my own child, I felt I had to find the courage to confront Mother. To try and get her to own up to her behavior. I tried to express my frustration at the way Mother behaved, at her selfishness and her self-centeredness. I didn't speak about her drinking or quick-boiling anger. But Mother saw through my attempts at calm, rational confrontation. She heard the truth behind my dissembling words, my sotto voce, my don't-disturb-the-baby tone. She cranked it up to eleven and immediately shouted that if I was telling her she had been a bad mother she would kill herself. Then she turned to Sara and asked her if she felt the same way I did. (I wondered if Sara's relationship with Mother was as fraught as I said mine was.) To my astonishment Sara said yes. (I wondered if Sara thought she was a bad mother.) Sara started to say, "Well . . ." and then stopped.

Erika demurred to answer altogether and for decades Mother clung to her youngest daughter as proof that she had been a good mother. Sara and I spent the next many years suffering Mother's huge silences and deep sighs whenever we saw her. After the blow up, we made our own tenuous peace treaties with her. But Erika waited and waited, doing her own poisonous dance with Mother and then, a couple of years before we knew Mother was sick, Erika sent an angry letter. The letter left no time for Mother—her mind already compromised although we did not know that—to get beyond what she saw as yet another betrayal by yet another daughter. The last one.

I got an email from Mother that started, *Do you know what your sister Erika did?* As if I hadn't been the one to throw the first punch; Erika's uppercut that knocked Mother down came so long after the initial jab that she seemed to have forgotten she could not trust me. Then, as now, when the shit hit the fan, I could not decide if Erika regretted having been finally honest or wished she had never mustered the courage.

It was sad and almost unkind to both Mother and Erika that my youngest sister waited so long to tell Mother the truth. I think perhaps Erika waited because she couldn't bear to think her relationship with Mother was as much a failure as Sara's and mine. Erika was a Pollyanna: She still believed in miracles; she truly thought people might change; she had faith in goodness. Her philosophy might have been influenced by the fact that she hadn't had as much disappointment in love as Sara or me: Sara's series of bad girlfriends; my marriage that had seemed so right but turned out so wrong—very early into it, although I never shared that with my sisters or my mother. Or with anyone, really. And they didn't know because my husband and I did not shout, we did not publicly disagree. And despite early and continuous misgivings, I had an intense desire to simply stay married at all costs. Despite my huge unhappiness I had a sick desire to show my parents how little I had really been affected by living among the detritus of their marriage. Their train wreck of a marriage which had rained debris down on all below them. I held on by sheer force of will even as my therapist pointed out, more than once that, "One person simply cannot do all the heavy lifting."

But Erika managed to make what looked, at first glance or even second, like a complete mismatch a truly successful marriage. At least from the outside, the only place I could view it from. It had taken me a long time to warm up to Erika's husband, Peter, and the truth was we would never really like each other, could only treat each other with the kind of cautious respect and care of a cat and a dog circling each other, but he treated my sister well and she seemed happy and that, I finally understood, was about as far as my stake in her business went. They showed the world a true Happy Families happy family.

From the outside, it seemed Erika had traveled the farthest from our youth by creating her own alternate universe, and so, I always wondered why she continued to endure further years of Mother's visits to her home, with their fits, tantrums, drunkenness and insults. Why had Erika been so unwilling to confront Mother's destructiveness? Why did she continue to allow Mother to toss grenades at her when I had put a stop to that, or at least a stop to my acknowledging it, many years earlier? I wondered if she still believed in happy families at any cost.

I think it was Erika's husband, Peter, who finally, at nearly the eleventh hour, gave Erika an ultimatum: He said he couldn't bear to see what Mother was doing to Erika. No more visits, he said, if they couldn't resolve things. He was fine, he said, with never seeing Mother again. He could not stand to have his home and his life disrupted, to watch his wife in tears and trembling with anger. He felt the guilt of the witness.

My ex-husband, Ben, had issued a similar ultimatum to me, earlier in our marriage. Ben watched the way Mother treated me and was confounded; he watched the way I took it and was pissed. He didn't understand why I spent so much time with her. Even if it eventually became clear to him that Mother and I had our dance and the two of us knew well the moves, he hated the entire number, loathed it down to the individual notes of the individual songs. I did, too. I did. But it wasn't until years later that I finally, furious, sad, but unwavering, changed the music and altered the dance with my mother so that we could bear to be in the same room for more than a few hours.

But by time Peter issued his ultimatum, Mother's age, drinking and infirmity had begun to spiral out of control and was taking a terrible toll. She was both more and less herself. She seemed angry all the time. Or sad. Or something as far from happy as I could imagine. Later, of course, I wondered: What did she suspect? Did she suspect? And when? How much of the last couple of years before the diagnosis did she spend trying to pretend that nothing was really wrong? Mother was a product of the Red Queen effect I had read about: She kept running as fast as she could just to keep up. And her disease would ensure that she did that for the rest of her life, only as the Alzheimer's progressed, running as fast as she could only put Mother farther and farther behind.

Too late for any good to come of it, Erika was finally honest in her letter, telling Mother that she could not continue to come to her home and abuse her. Erika's letter to Mother achieved the same result as my words years before, although, perhaps, with less fury and more injured silence. And the betrayal inherent in that silence lasted right up until the time Mother got sick. She never forgave Erika for being the last, the final of her daughters, to turn on her.

When Erika realized she was not going to achieve anything like the result she imagined, wanted, needed, she reverted to her role as perfect and dutiful daughter, visiting Mother once a week, taking her out for lunch, trying to shop with her. But inside, Erika was still a woman trying to come to terms with the truth that Mother was a mean, sick drunk. And perhaps she wished she had acknowledged it earlier. Or perhaps she wished she had never, ever acknowledged it.

6.

At two points in her life, separated by many years, my mother coalesced at Sanderstone. The first time, Hannah checked her in when Mother had her nervous breakdown. She had been found catatonic and in bed by her best friend. The second, we, the kids, checked her in because she needed to dry out. We had wanted her to get sober so that we might all be able to carve out a few good years toward the end, to try one last time to rescue Mother from herself. To assuage our own guilt at our neglect of her. Mother was pushed, not completely unwilling, into rehab. She, too, knew she wasn't herself so she acquiesced, finally. We all felt so strongly that Mother had to get sober. She simply had to. It might not help everything, it might not help *anything*, but there was some value in the last attempt to change the old order. If only so we could just say we had done everything we could. And then. It didn't matter.

We understood the irony of this return to Sanderstone. We got the cruelty of it. But there were few choices. We should have been first alert to the fact that Mother really was at the end of her own pretense when she actually *agreed* to return to Sanderstone. For years, just driving past the place would make her shudder. She would make detours to avoid the discreet gates that led up the long hill. We should have known at that moment that she was fearful something terrible had happened—if she was willing to admit that she drank a *little* too much, if she was willing to seek help in a place that had been the stuff of her worst nightmares. But as I walked Mother into Sanderstone and held her hand in mine, she said only: "I have been here before?" I held her hand tighter and it shook. She could not remember *why* she had been here. I remained silent remembering the last time she was immobile and unresponsive. I compared that version of Mother to the broken and terrified and desperate Mother before me. I understood the question in Mother's voice. A place that had loomed so large in my own consciousness for so many years seemed so much smaller, so much more benign than the image in my head.

I was the only one of her daughters who went to visit during that first incarceration. I was twenty-two and living in Boston, and I went with my bubbe who sat in the car tearing tissues into tiny pieces until she could get out of the car without crying. Erika and Sara had not been able to bring themselves to come at all, something for which Mother never forgave them. However, Mother had a list of unforgivable acts: impugning her motherhood in any way, big or small; throwing a tantrum; accusing her of making *ash aun porkh*, ashes and dust, of the dinner she prepared. Ashes and dust.

The patients at Sanderstone wandered the halls in their pajamas, dazed and unsure, as though they had been called down for a fire drill and were waiting further instructions. *Farmisht*. Mixed up, confused, crazy. I took a mother I did not recognize out to lunch. She pushed her egg salad around the plate, but this was nothing new: She was a woman who would remove the insides of bagels and then just nibble at the shells. But she herself was unfamiliar: too thin even for her own vanity, what she would have called skin and bones. She was dressed in clothes that could not be hers, a harbinger of things to come. Her eyes were hollowed out; there was no energy in them; she seemed so much more than depressed; she had lost the core strength that had kept her going for more than fifty years. Yet a few months after her first stay at Sanderstone, we had most of our more familiar Mother back.

But the second stay was different. She remained sober for a few weeks, but she fought against her drinking as a problem, and she whined that we all were making a huge deal about nothing. And then she was diagnosed with Alzheimer's.

For the most part, she didn't acknowledge her condition. She never ever said that word: *Alzheimer's*. There was a small part of her that truly believed she could go back to the before times. To her version of normal, even if she couldn't exactly describe what that normal was or how it would bear out. Mostly it seemed she was nostalgic for the time before things fell apart. That would have meant some spectacular wizardry, a complete rebirth beginning at her womb.

Yet, even as she pushed back a little, whined about going home, seemed to think this was all a bit silly, Mother—a woman who completed the Sunday *New York Times* crossword puzzle in ink every week, who read voraciously, who prided herself on her education, her erudition, who was a veritable and predictable literary snob who wanted so desperately to write something big, important, acclaimed, who was a woman who adored opera, the theater, movies, who maneuvered a conversation as well as an Edward Albee character—really just gave up.

I watched her intellectual disintegration with trepidation. Her mind was her best part, cruel and ugly as it could be. It was my best part, too, in, I hoped, a more gentle, kinder way. I had always been convinced that, were I given the choice, I would rather live without my body than my mind. If I had my mind I could read, watch movies, think. The loss of movement would be devastating but the loss of my mind seemed unfathomable. Still, I wondered about that choice at the moment of Mother's decline.

I was in the middle of a divorce. I had a lover who had reintroduced me to the joys of sex in middle age. I began to reconsider giving up that body. It was all an exercise in what ifs. And, if this, then that. But that is what you do when a loved one gets sick with a terrible, terminal disease. You can't help but wonder how you'd fare if it was you; how would you cope? What deals would you make with God? Would you lose faith or regain its strength? At the same moment that I lost my mother I found myself. I knew I had the courage to leave my marriage, to risk my future, to upend Ivy's comfort, with all the good and bad inherent in that decision. And yet I watched a woman who had never been okay with much of anything be resigned to, seemingly fine with, a world-scorching diagnosis that would destroy the two things about herself she valued most: her brains and her beauty. She sat back into Alzheimer's and let it wrap around her like a beanbag chair.

She was too far gone, Mother, due to her dishonesty, our blindness and neglect, to make any other decision. It was far too late for Mother to take matters into her own hands. She and I had never talked about her future; she had never told any of us what she wanted. She knew her own mother had succumbed to dementia and while my bubbe's descent was prettier than Mother's, as far as I knew, Mother must have understood, on some level, the huge downward slope. Pre-diagnosis, if I had to bet on a reaction, I would have said suicide. She had, after all, been threatening that much of her life. But she did not even consider that option and I had no idea if she *could* any longer. I had no idea how much of her rational mind was left. Like so many other intimacies she refused to share with her daughters, she was keeping this last one close to her chest.

A month after Mother was diagnosed Erika and I moved

her out of her house and into the assisted living facility with a memory unit: *Menuchat Lev*. She half-heartedly fought it for a while; she cried every time one of us dropped her off at the home that was not her house; she complained about the food, she told everyone that she had moved to *Menuchat Lev* just because she could no longer drive. She said everyone around her had something wrong with them, everyone was old. These things were all mostly true. Yet Mother could not hold on to her anger, she couldn't nurse it as she had when she was younger and healthier. It flashed and then it was gone. There were even moments of clarity when she was grateful, or seemed so, that she no longer had to pretend to be competent; it seemed a relief for her to give up the charade of being normal.

And Mother, dry for months, began drinking again with a vengeance. She didn't understand the point of staying sober. We tried to tell her that the Aricept, then a new drug meant to slow down the progress of the disease, wouldn't work as well if she drank excessively. We all tried to talk to her, and then Hannah, Sara and I pretty much gave up. Erika alone was insistent Mother stop drinking.

She said to me, "*You* don't have to put up with this all the time. *You're* just visiting her for a few days, a week. You fly up and see her and then you fly back and forget her." That wasn't a bit true, but I understood my sister's fury when she said, "*You* don't have to deal with her drinking every time you take her to lunch or dinner, *you* don't have to stop and buy a bottle every time you take her back home."

That was a fact. Sara and I lived down South. Erika was an hour and a half away, and therefore the one on call, so to speak, when things went bad. And they did, for several years. Safely ensconced in her spacious apartment with no car and no way to do too much damage to others, Mother just drank. The director of the residence called and told us she had fallen or misbehaved or would not get out of bed. *Something.* We dealt with it by taking away Mother's credit cards, refusing her the glass of wine when we took her out to lunch, warning the residence not to serve her during their happy hours. We were terrified she would be asked to leave. We worried as much about her drinking as her memory. But a drunk will drink.

I sympathized with Erika but that first summer, just a couple of months after her diagnosis, when I was trapped in a tiny cottage desperately trying to give Mother one more decent moment, I didn't think cheap wine was the hill to die on. I thought it was the least I could do. Allowing Mother to drink was a small price to pay when I had paid much larger prices in the past: all the visits for all the decades, all the passive-aggressive criticism, all the huge hysteria, all the days she was locked in her room. Growing up essentially motherless had been awful, yes, but I was over it. It was done. I was grown and more.

7.

All possibilities exist at any moment, but when I first learned of a test I could take that would possibly reveal my chances of losing my mind to Alzheimer's, I could not even wrap my head around the *idea* of test. I couldn't bear the knowledge of an outcome like Mother's while I was still processing hers. Now that scientists seem to come up with new ways to predict our genetic fate, I wonder if I will eventually succumb all the time. I wonder what it would mean to know, how it would affect my relationships. I wonder, too, if I had known what was going to happen to Mother, would I have played the whole relationship with her differently? Had I known for sure she had a finite time of the mind, would I have been more honest, less angry? Could I have forgiven her sooner?

Mother had the habit of repeating all her lies over and over so that they began to look like truths: we were bad, spoiled, ungrateful children. We made her miserable. We didn't love her as we should have. We were distant and uncaring. We used our feelings to punish her. None of those things were true in the main, but as I grew older and older, I did understand that they were a part of her self-fulfilling prophecy. She thought we were bad, so we were.

I have also read that honesty is only the *habit* of repeating something over and over so in that case even a lie can *become* a truth. If I said to Mother endlessly, *I love you, I love you. I love you*, would that have made a difference in the end? Would it have turned into a truth? Would it have stopped the lies and evil words? Would we be able to be in the same room without maiming each other?

If I had known her fate would I have used the last good years she had left to try and force a true rapprochement? Would it have even been possible? From the vantage point of middle age, I wish I had said to her, as I did to my daughter each time she struck out at me: *I love you. I love you. I love you.* But would it, could it have diffused Mother's fury like it stopped my daughter's tantrums in their tracks? Could I have shaped our lives differently?

Reality is what refuses to go away when you don't believe in it: I heard that somewhere, too. We could wish and wish that things were different, could *still* be different, but the truth was, the reality was, my mother was gone. Mother as I knew her had been carted away—another victim, draped on the heap of the legion of other victims of that plague. I could pretend differently. Most of the time, when I looked into Mother's eyes there was nothing left behind them: It was as if her hard drive had crashed, most of the memory had been lost and what *was* left was corrupted. A permanent error message would appear. She might have known this somehow because for the first three or so years of the illness she wore the dark glasses she had always affected *out* of doors, inside, too. She said her eyes hurt. Her eyes hurt me too.

I could ignore the obvious. I could suspend belief. I could put my faith in whomever, whatever. Or nothing. I could *believe* anything I wished. But if I could believe *in* something enough that it gave comfort, could I dismiss the power of something I chose *not* to believe in? What would the scientists who study belief have to say? Was it even possible? Probably not. We believe what we wish to believe, and what we choose not to accept loses all meaning: We divorce ourselves from its existence. Mother and I had no way to go but forward into our new lives, into whatever level of consciousness that presented itself.

Science is doing wonderful things in dissecting our brains, but will science ever catch up to what we *think* we know? Will it ever be able to help discriminate between a shared or common belief and evidence, hard evidence that might disprove all of everything, even itself? Until such time as that happens, if ever, we exist on faith and hope and desire, with despair and sadness and anger and fear crowding in. Mother's life was nourished in bitterness; she saw everywhere she was as just another shtetl, as just another place in which she was trapped. Everywhere she went, she wanted to vacate; then she mourned leaving but would not consider return.

The older I got, the more pleasure I took in the same ritualized events which once bored me as a child and younger woman. I took comfort in going to synagogue, listening to the prayers, the rabbi, letting it all take me away, if for only a moment, from my awesome responsibilities. But why, I wondered? Why did I feel better? And why did I also find comfort in having a mother who was now known, who like a ritualized event, behaved the same way each time I saw her, who no longer turned and turned and spit words like the venom of a snake. Who no longer accused me of provoking her anger?

Do we really need to touch the stove to know how hot it is, how badly it can burn?

The fifty years of my life before Mother's diagnosis were, I knew, but a tiny second, and the years from then on would move even faster. If the covenant of God was based on a bestowal of blessing in exchange for His appreciation, then I was okay with that. I could thank whoever, or no one, that there was a tiny peace in the tragedy of my mother.

Sara would have none of it. She said, "I find little comfort in anything these days." She focused on the pragmatic. "What I think is that this dealing with Mother now is just like work. Like a bad job, one you just don't want to even get out of bed for. I feel dutiful but there's little pleasure in it.

On the other hand," Sara had the grace to smile, "being with Mother has always been that way."

"You're right," I admitted. "It's true. What pleasure there has ever been in being with Mother has always been fleeting and somehow inauthentic. And now we can't even get angry at her. It wouldn't matter if we did. Nothing would come of it. There is not the tiniest iota of hope that we'll ever be able to talk to her about what happened in the past. There is no way to ever get any answers from the questions we were always too afraid to ask. That hope is gone forever. Mother, as we ever knew her, is gone. Bringing up the past to a woman who has no short-term memory is more than cruel. But, if she has any long-term memory left, and I suspect she does, then she knows exactly what she has done in the past. She may not know enough to ask us to forgive her. But I would think she hopes that we don't abandon her for it."

"I think that somehow she is *sure* we won't abandon her, even as she weeps every time we leave," Sara said angrily back at me. "There has always been an assurance about her that any abandonment by us is merely temporary. She is arrogant that way. And she's right. No matter how many times we leave, she reels us back. And the rewards, like that bad job you go to day after day, are so fucking small. A ten-cent raise after ten years. With Mother it has always been impossible to know what she is thinking, especially about us. And impossible to know if we are ever doing anything right."

But, try as I might, I could not share Sara's anger. Yes, it was agonizing watching the push and pull between the

SHIVAH

Mother who had been and the Mother who was. Yes, it was hard to accept at each visit what was really left of her: to watch the moments when her eyes cleared for a second and she seemed both lost *and* found. I knew then that the longer the illness lasted, the worse she would get. I thought I was prepared.

There would come a day when Mother was finally able to remember nothing but the absolute present moment; her confusion, her anger, her sadness dissipated forever. But mine would not take root. I was angry at what had happened to Mother, I was furious at God and the world, but by the time she died, I had been watching her leave for so long that I finally allowed myself to properly mourn her. At the end of her life, fifteen years after the diagnosis, as we watched the death rattle from her throat, I understood that this loss was the most profound.

8.

What separates the ordinary, normal act of forgetting from the seeds that will bloom into the complete loss of memory? If changes begin in midlife or even earlier, how do we monitor them without giving over our present to the preservation of both a past and a future?

When reason is gone, when we are without it, who are we really? Was Mother locked someplace inside and had just forgotten the key? Or was there nothing left inside at all? Had the safe been emptied completely of its contents? When life's meaning goes from a whoosh to a dribble, what is left? What is life? What is the meaning of existence?

Doctors have said that there can be a very long phase when people are not themselves. They are no longer recognizable to their loved ones. My problem was that Mother had been so many selves, to herself and us, to her husband, her friends, even her grandchildren. I had little idea which Mother it was who *wasn't* her *self*. The gorgeous, literate party girl? The actress? The melancholy feminist? The hoarder? The pecunious woman who cried poverty? The distant mother? The harpy? The shrew? The woman who stroked the tender inside of my arm when I wordlessly put it out there? Who stayed up with me all night when I couldn't breathe? The reader? The writer? The woman who played Leonard Cohen's "Suzanne" on the piano? The woman who encouraged and discouraged all at a moment's notice? The woman whose sickness I didn't understand until it became meaningless? I didn't know which Mother I was losing. I didn't know which Mother to grieve. And it is grief, not hope that is the thing with feathers: spreading its wings, flapping, flapping in larger and larger circles, gathering in everything around it.

9.

In hindsight it was terribly naïve of all of us to think that we could get Mother sober after more than forty years, and that she really could start over. We were naïve and intrusive. And ridiculous. We essentially tricked her into rehab, Mother complicit because for at least two years she had suspected she was sick. And so by the time *she* figured it out, we figured it out. Then Mother was sober, and then. And then. And then.

In the beginning, a small part of me felt as if I had caused the Alzheimer's by demanding she get sober. Had we all left her to her own devices, might she have just drunk herself away from herself instead of Alzheimer's doing it for her? Could we have accepted that? Perhaps. We all had moments when we imagined her falling down the stairs or wrecking her car. But we didn't have to accept an accidental demise like that. The diagnosis forced our hands. Now all we could do was accept the consequences.

The real problem was never Mother's drinking, anyway.

It just seemed the thing that might be the easiest to control. The real problem was the mental illness that had been illustrated by Mother's chronic unhappiness and her urgent need to self-medicate, to mitigate, to keep the demons that plagued her at bay. Half a century ago, a diagnosis of bipolar disorder might have been difficult for the doctors to offer and equally impossible for Mother to accept. Housewives were just generally crazy, weren't they? Especially smart Jewish ones set down in the rural South, a foreign land for sure. Even if a diagnosis had been made, Mother's resistance to a description of any mental disorder other than slight depression or anxiety just meant that no one need look close enough for the truth. The fact is that we all just accepted that she was different.

Her own mother, my bubbe, had handled Mother with kid gloves since childhood, Hannah told me more than once. Mother was the difficult one. She had always been hard to manage. As a child, I overheard my father describe Mother as high strung but no one had ever offered a further explanation as to why she spent weeks in bed, or why she suddenly got up in a fury and left the dinner table. I have very clear memories of walking into my parent's room one evening and seeing Mother stretched out on the bed, weeping into a pillow while my darkly handsome Father rubbed the backs of her legs with lotion. At the expense of his children, Father spent his entire marriage trying to soothe her.

When I was in my forties, before Mother got sick, I tried to confront my father about his enabling of Mother, about the way he left his three daughters in the care of a woman he knew wasn't stable. He went off to work each day and left us with a woman who just couldn't cope. Naturally, my father resisted the discussion. He said he had done the best that he could. But I was never satisfied with that response.

And even after the breakdown, after she was under a psychiatrist's care and taking Prozac for what would be nearly two decades, when we understood that Mother's primary disorder was organic, it was still easy to use her drinking as a more facile explanation for some or another cruel outburst or peculiar behavior. *She simply could not help herself.* She, too, was doing the best she could, right?

We found, in a way, that she was not doing the best she could. Her shrink was a charlatan who bought her charade as easily as too many others had. He medicated her with antidepressants instead of digging deeper. He believed Mother's stories about what terrible children she had: how much the three of us took her for granted, how we had ruined any chance she ever had for a real life, how unappreciated and unloved she was. We were easy bad guys. He was charmed.

Her doctor had no idea how much she was drinking or if she was drinking at all because Mother lied as smoothly as a young child saying, "I didn't do it. It wasn't me," when all evidence pointed to the contrary. Surely the psychiatrist couldn't have known about her drinking or he would have tried to stop her, right? Wouldn't he have known that the antidepressants he prescribed would do nothing as long as she continued to self-medicate? Of course. But for nearly twenty years Mother paid the doctor to tell her she was right, and he took her checks and wrote her scrips and nodded at her tales of woe.

I know antidepressants can only do so much, they are not magic. But they can keep your head above water while you at least try and learn to swim. Mother's wrong dose of, wrong kind of medication barely kept her head above water most days; it was as if she spent most of her life choking on water while she thrashed her hands and feet to keep herself moving. If anything, Mother got worse. Even if she occasionally swam fast and strong, her life was more drowning than waving.

I read a story in which a mentally ill patient refused to acknowledge that she was mentally ill and then refused treatment. Because the woman lacked what doctors and therapists called "insight," which was defined ambiguously eighty years ago in the DSM as "the correct attitude to a morbid change in oneself," she would accept no diagnosis or help that defined her as mentally unstable. Did Mother lack that same insight? Perhaps.

She hadn't been quite unstable enough to be institutionalized for more than a few weeks when she had her breakdown and was committed to Sanderstone the first time, but there was clearly nothing normal, ordinary, or easy about her moods. They made it impossible to tell, one day to the next, which Mother would be present. As children we saw that she was unpredictable, angry, sad, withdrawn. As adults, we found her anger more pointed. We were the ones regularly subjected to that fury. Her anger could still leave me shaking in my boots because there was both no way to predict it and no tried-and-true way to diffuse it. She'd decide my home wasn't clean enough or she'd tell my daughter, Ivy, she didn't have to eat her supper, that I wasn't serious. She'd leave every restaurant table to conveniently go the bathroom right before the check was brought. Then she'd forget to thank whoever had picked it up. She sent used things as gifts, forgot birthdays, said Ivy's Hanukkah requests were too extravagant. None of these things in themselves were awful; it was just the years and years of buildup. The knowledge that nothing we did would be enough, never mind make her happy for a few moments. There was this hot, simmering stew beneath her words and actions and we had no idea when or why it would spill over.

No, it wasn't Mother's drinking as self-medication that was the problem. The drinking was her response to something, anything, that frightened or unnerved her: something with which she could not cope. There was a lot of that. She couldn't cope with noise from children or music that was too loud. She couldn't cope with being asked for anything, but equally, she could not bear being ignored. She needed to be the life of every party, except when she didn't. She needed so desperately to be appreciated every moment for anything she did. And just as often, she wanted to be left alone.

SHIVAH

I could mark those occasions when Mother's being drunk seemed like the problem, but it never really quite was. At the huge campus dance the night before my college graduation, Mother and her scotch had a running start before I even met up with her and my father. My date, an older man recently separated and with young children, had cancelled at the last moment. There I stood, all dressed up and thinking I was all grown up but with no promised handsome lover to show off, while Mother was too drunk to even notice I didn't have a companion. I was never sure exactly why she had chosen that particular crucially important event in my life to get roaring. Was it because I was doing something fun and exciting, starting a new life, something Mother could not bear to watch sober? Was it just the same old garden-variety unhappiness that had been her lot for so long? I didn't know then that her own marriage was crumbling into pieces at that very moment, but there were clues.

A scant year after my graduation Mother had her breakdown. I don't think that fully explained her selfishness that evening or why she had no compunction about ruining my evening. Over a lifetime it became clear that no matter what occasion was being celebrated, whose tragedy was being mourned, every commemoration, every bad or good thing that happened to anyone and everyone else was really all about Mother.

The Ceremony of the Washing of the Hands

Cleaning one's hands after a burial is connected to the ancient belief that demons hover around the dead.

Washing one's hands during mourning separates the mitzvah of honoring the dead from that of comforting the bereaved.

1.

When I was a little girl, six or seven, I used to spend afternoons after school in Mother's bathroom while she bathed. She had the odd habit all of her life of washing her underwear and bras in the bathwater as she soaked. The bath was a daily ritual; an hour before my father got home, she would draw the bath and soak with her underthings. Then she would dress, comb out her hair, reapply her makeup, including bright red lipstick. The first time I saw the actress Gena Rowlands paint her lips scarlet in the film *A Woman Under the Influence* I felt like I had fallen through the looking glass. *Mother.*

Mother knew exactly how much time she had to get ready and she also knew that her husband was rarely, if ever, late. The afternoon ritual was a performance—both the actors and the audience would be ready well before curtain—and the clothes she chose for each occasion could only have been called costumes. She loved to dress up. She loved to look whatever part she was playing. She had her housewife costume, her luncheon costume, her dinner party costume, her errand-running costume, and the more elaborate costumes she wore when giving a party. She was a throwback to the elegant past when people changed clothes several times a day and put on a fancy dress for dinner, even though she had grown up lower middle class with nothing extra and no luxury.

Mother had two closets full of fashionable clothes. She had suits and high heels. She had evening gowns and cocktail dresses and pantsuits and everything in between. She had outfits for every occasion and for every time the fashions changed or the era upended itself sartorially. Her bathroom had enough potions and lotions and makeup and scents for a department store counter.

But her disguises ran to much more than mere clothing and paint. She was the queen of subterfuge: in the way she laced her iced tea or orange juice with vodka. She was the diva of confusion: in the way she could make crying sound like laughing, pain like love. She had the power to make an ordinary dinner a wondrous event or, just as likely, the last night on the Titanic.

It was never possible at any given moment to know which Mother would appear out of the bedroom or bath, which Mother would drive into the driveway, which Mother would wake up in the morning, which Mother would walk down the hall, which Mother would show up at the dinner table. They were *all* ours, though, all those Mothers. They were the only ones we had. So we adjusted our behavior accordingly as best we could. On very short notice.

By the early seventies, my mother and father grew more casual with the times and Mother more careless in her dressing. Gone were the high heels and suits, the slim skirts. Mother happily bought and wore blue jeans, tie-dyed tops and scarves, acres and acres of scarves; she was well aware that her thin, angular body looked dramatic and yet unstudied in the clothes of that time. People always told her how young she looked. My father grew his hair long, and Mother wrapped hers in a bandana. As teenagers we shied away from them as was the normal course of things: They embarrassed us. But we had always been wary of our parents; we had never trusted them for more than a moment at a time anyway. If they transformed themselves into hippies before our eyes (even as we wore the same outfits), they remained beautifully pathetic. They were still the same people *inside*: Father distant and preoccupied by work, Mother crazy, drunk, sad, challenging. The emotional abuse continued unabated as we grew, even if it was dressed in a different costume.

Mother's new image was as crystal clear to her as her other incarnations, but if she could bend to the times in fashion, her core personality never changed its course. She continued to bounce from saint to sinner, sane to nuts, weepy to furious, with no outward bruises to show for it. Yet as a concussion rattles the brain in the head and may bring on dementia dozens of years later, her careening from persona to persona and back again rattled her brain too. Who knows if that past was partially responsible for her future?

By the age of fifty, Mother had left my father, had a nervous breakdown, recovered and begun a new life. As she grew older and retired in her late sixties, her interest in clothes waned; she didn't want to spend money on things like that. She was more eager to spend it on travel, gobbling up new countries like her grandchildren did Cheerios. When Erika and I cleaned out Mother's closet as we moved her from her house to assisted living many of Mother's clothes literally fell apart in our hands. And yet for several years after the diagnosis, Mother kept up appearances. She wore lipstick and some of her costume jewelry.

Even six years after Mother went to *Menuchat Lev*, Hannah would call me after a visit with Mother and say, "Your mother looked beautiful. She still dresses every day." That mattered more to Hannah than to me. Hannah seemed to feel that as long as Mother looked good on the outside, the decay on the inside was slowed. It gave her hope that her sister wasn't really slipping away. Hannah needed her sister to be as she had been, and it was true that if one did not look too carefully, too closely, for too long, Mother did retain some small semblance of her long-ago glamour. It was enough to fool someone who did not know her, but it should not have given hope to those who did. There were the occasional flashes of the old Mother: She'd snap or make a sarcastic remark, she'd stop and preen in front of the mirror. She had been a very beautiful woman and been well aware of it; it made sense that her vanity was one of the last things to go.

So for the first couple of years, we all tried our best

to maintain appearances. It was as if her gently crumbling exterior would make it too easy for us to let her go, to help us cope with the eventual total loss of her, so even though she hated it and we hated it when we were with her, Erika or Hannah or I would take her shopping. Mother would grow weary after less than an hour and beg to go home, at the same time she would insist that she needed things, important things: bras and lipstick and shows and always shoes.

Erika took Mother to the huge mall downtown where she had Mother try on every pair of black flats at Nordstrom's, Clarks, and Naturalizer. None of them fit, Mother insisted. Hundreds of pairs and none of them suited her.

"It's just her way of keeping control," Sara told me when Erika reported yet another failure. "She's saying: You can't *make* me buy shoes, and I won't let you."

"That's ridiculous," I answered. I had a hard time believing Mother's astonishing ability to manipulate had survived the ravages of the disease. She'd been formidable as a wild animal, yes, one that we dared poke only once before she bit us, but surely, surely, she had lost her claws, her bite? She had not. Yet.

Months later, on a visit with Mother, I was pressed into taking Mother around to stores: Nordstrom's again, Macy's, others, and still she could not find a pair of shoes that fit.

"It's this toe," Mother said, pointing out a toe that stuck slightly up.

"Well, then, that's that," I said giving up immediately. I knew Hannah or Erika would have argued with her, but I knew that whether it was conscious or just the vestiges of old behavior, it wouldn't do me any good to force her. It would not do her any good, either. Fighting with a woman with dementia in a shopping mall? I had a sudden recall of such public arguments, and I had no wish to repeat them. In the early years, Mother's disease was a constant sword of Damocles. And very sharp.

When Erika called me to find out if we had bought shoes, I told her, "No. Mother couldn't find any. Finally I stopped even trying. We just sat and had a coffee. She really doesn't seem to want shoes, much as she needs them. And I couldn't keep taking her from store to store. It seems cruel to force her to shop. You know she has always hated shopping. Doing it now seems like we're trying to punish her when she doesn't have the mental strength to stop us."

"But all of her shoes are old and ruined. They're falling apart," Erika protested. "It was silly of you to just give up."

"Perhaps. But it still seemed mean to drag her from place to place. I just couldn't do it."

Mother watched me from the sofa we had bought all in a rush with the other furniture in her new place, all bought and delivered the same day we knew she had a place to live. "Who was that?" she asked as I put my phone back in my purse.

"Erika," I said.

"What did she want?"

"Nothing."

Mother sat and read the front section of the *Provi-*

dence Journal for the fifth time that day. She looked up at me. "Who were you talking to?"

"Erika," I said.

"What did she want?"

"She wanted to know if we had bought you some new shoes," I said.

"Did we?" Mother asked.

"No," I said.

"Good," Mother said. "I don't need any shoes."

"Right," I said.

Admittedly, on my visits, I just wanted a little peace and quiet, something that had eluded all of us for too many years. Mother was calmer now that she had lost her mind and if the price to pay for some semblance of order was letting Mother wear worn-out shoes, so be it. A man once said to me that in life we coast awhile and we pedal awhile. I had been pedaling for a very long time; I was enjoying taking my feet off the pedals and just letting the bike take me where it would.

2.

The second summer after Mother's diagnosis, the last ever at the beach house, I brought my lover, Paul, to the cottage when I went with her. I had separated from Ben, a long time coming, but oddly in sync with Mother's diagnosis. So two things I had let go of: old Mother, old marriage.

Even in the midst of mourning my mother's disease I was selfishly, deliriously happy. It was ironic that my separation occurred at nearly the same age as my mother's from my father, but it hadn't sent me to my bed or into a mental hospital. It made clear to me that even if happiness was not the choice I wished it were, I still had the capacity for it, no matter how large the odds stacked against me were.

As I watched Mother give in to the loss of her mind, I became sanguine about my own losses. Can you miss what you no longer have? Is the loss of something that is no longer at all attainable really a loss at all? Rousseau posits that essentially happiness is the feeling of existence, a "resting place" for the soul, where it need not be engaged in past or present.

If that feeling persists, he says, we can indeed call ourselves happy. When I looked at Mother, New Mother, dissolved memory Mother, I felt that maybe she was actually there in a Rousseau-esque limbo, in that world between the past and the present. That was where she lived and where she would die. So wasn't it possible that Mother was truly happy for the first time in her life?

I knew Paul in high school; we dated passionately but also desultorily. We were very young, and we were sure of everything and nothing. Both of us were seeking ways out of our lives but weren't even sure what that meant. He had been around Mother a bit and remembered her as a beautiful, glamorous, and dramatic force who commanded a room. He thought my life as close to perfect as possible: two handsome parents, a big modern house, money, privilege. He was stunned when I began to tell him stories of how it really was to be my mother's daughter. No one my sisters and I grew up with knew anything different than Paul; we had kept it all inside. You didn't talk about that sort of thing back then, and anyway, everyone's parents were stupid and uncool, impossible in every way: How were we to know there was anything special or different about ours?

To Paul, the transformation of Mother from how she was in his memory to where she was that summer—essentially an invalid who was losing her mind and had to be shepherded about, a woman, soft and fuzzy around the edges, who needed constant attentive babying—was a shock. But he was not unaccustomed to death. His parents were both gone of long and debilitating illnesses. Hearing about the needy side of Mother was the only unsettling information for him. He didn't expect that as sick as she was, Mother could still be crafty and manipulative; if her manipulations had lost most of their edge and purpose, the vestiges, like her vanity, peeked out unexpectedly.

    I spent hours telling Paul all the stories of Old Mother before he was exposed to New Mother. I prepared him. He said he was glad she was gone; he was sorry she had hurt me. But as I talked, I realized I no longer felt hurt, hadn't in a while. There was something dispassionate but honest in the stories; it was as if I were describing someone I used to know. It was true in a sense. Neither Mother nor I were people we had formerly been. In some important ways, I had been changed as much as she. Her letting her *self* go meant I had two choices. I could continue to be with her in the ways I had always been— alternately angry, hurt, damaged. I could react in any of the myriad ways I had in the past. Or I could start treating her as the new person she now was. Mostly harmless, needy, tragic. My life with her had gone from a domestic novel to an epic. I had to behave accordingly.

In an article about mental illness—when I still read such things, when I didn't know what Mother had, when I thought our future's trajectory could be changed—I stopped at the line: "Freedom often ends up looking a lot like abandonment." But for me the sentence was turned around. I had felt abandoned by my mother my whole life. Then, the literal abandonment felt like freedom. Because Mother had always been like a mutation of Glinda and the Wicked Witch of the East. She was the mistress of both delight and deceit. So very, very good. So very, very bad. Accordingly, my sisters and I always trod carefully around her, as if we walked on smooth, round glass marbles that could shatter at any moment into shards that would lance and bloody our feet and render us immobile.

So much of my youth and early adulthood I felt like I had been unable to move at all, unable to decide whether to go forwards or backwards, to continue or retreat. Like that childhood game of statues, I stood as still as I could and hoped Mother would not even notice the moment in which, in my exhaustion and helplessness, I might move a muscle, twitch an eye, stumble forward. Caught. She did notice us occasionally, even if she didn't then tend to us as a mother should. Or, later as we parsed her, as we decided a mother should. She wasn't like mothers in books. She wasn't kind. She wasn't selfless. She was beautiful, yes, admired, absolutely, and a bone-deep narcissist.

3.

In an alternate universe, somewhere in Hilbert space, an abstract yet infinite dimensional space—or perhaps in a parallel world like that which exists in the television show *Fringe* or the Bizarro world of Superman comics—is there a different Mother? Does there, in one of those places or another, rest a Mother who was able to properly love her children? In that place, did those children love her back? Was there a Mother who did not drink away her unhappiness, who did not write things like this in her journal?

> *Right now, I am experiencing an acute anxiety and an enormous fatigue, exhaustion so that putting one finger after another on the keys is too much. My chest tightened and it started just this morning at five thirty when I awoke knowing something awful was going to happen and I couldn't breathe. I want to sleep. I want to take something and go to*

SHIVAH

sleep but I am afraid I will stop breathing, that I will suffocate.

At some point, left alone in the house she had designed herself—my father had moved out, her children had flown the nest—Mother let happen the breakdown she had been teetering on for so many years, but not really consciously. One day she lay down and could not get up.

Could our universe hold both the mother I had and one who did not refuse to get help, who did not deny her mental illness and who did not blame her life's course on fate rather than forethought? Was there a Mother out there who took responsibility? Was there a Mother who was not sick? That sort of universe appealed to me, but in all probability, alternate universes, should they exist, are like the proverbial grass on the other side of the fence: greener until one gets down close.

Sure, Mother's life had been made complicated by us: three small children all in a row. We weren't what she expected. She thought us chaos agents—she pronounced us tummlers—but we were not the ones causing the chaos. She seemed to find us even as we stood like statues, trying not to get in her way. She would bark contradictory orders to move, stay, think, don't think, making it both impossible to play the game and inconceivable we could ever win.

For as long as I could remember she had doled out her affections as though they were finite, a box of expensive chocolates that would empty sooner or later. But she also doled out her criticisms and they were more prolific. And cheaper. The Torah tells us that evil words are worse than physical violence: They kill over and over. They hurt the person who says them, too, and anyone who overhears. Evil words are a sin against God and Mother had done her share of sinning.

When Paul had asked me how I had allowed Mother to be so powerful and to do so much damage for so long, I had no answer for him. I could no longer recall how painful it had been to still want something from Mother. To think I might get anything from her except anger and ugliness and pain. I had wished for her love, her approval, her friendship, her kindness for such a long, long time. Yet I had begun, even years before the Alzheimer's, to lower my expectations, to lower and lower and lower them. If, for too long, I had been willing to take any kind of bruising from her, if, for too long, I had kept getting back in the ring, bloodied and dazed, I finally had begun to realize that neither fighting back nor surrendering would get me anything close to what I wanted. The outcome would forever be the same: a temporary, uneasy truce for the sake of the grandchild and a permanent emotional estrangement. That is what I settled for without even continuing the battle. Paul told me he admired me for giving up the fight; he had faith in me to make the right choices now that she was sick. He had, I think, more faith in me that I had in myself. The disease still made me furious at times.

Not only had it robbed me of a resolution, it had robbed my mother of any kind of second chance—and I was a firm believer in second chances. After all she had remade herself once before.

If we are at our sickest with those to whom we are the closest then my sisters and I had both a seriously acute and a chronic illness from being the daughters of Mother. After all, we are all, in some way, disordered: We have just learned to live with whatever binds or blinds us. Mother's diagnosis gave me a sense of calm around her: There was no further expectation that she would shake off her own sickness, that she might see the error of her ways, become a different sort of person, love her children in ways we could understand and accept. In odd moments during the first couple of years, I still had vestiges of hope but then hope is what both leads us into despair and back out again. I gave it up.

The thing I grasped when I first heard the word *Alzheimer's*, but lost and had to grasp again and again, was that I would never, could never, have the kind of reconciliation with Mother made prominent in made-for-television movies or feel-good women's novels. There would be no final shouting, no final hug, no moment of ultimate forgiveness. There would be no real peace. The best that could be hoped for was a détente.

As soon as the doctor told us what was wrong with her, I knew I had to forgive her everything or I had to walk away forever. I could not walk away. Mother was in me; her bones were my bones, her chromosomes were entangled with mine. I was an egg she had carried her whole life. Her trauma was mine, too. We were an epigenetic mess: the dough rising before the kneading. Contained on all sides by a bowl we could easily soar out of, overflowing onto the counter. Everything that had happened to her had also happened to me. I was marked. I was coded. Anxiety, fear, depression, ennui. Creativity, beauty, trimness, a sense of the absurd. A love of flowers and reading. A distaste for small talk. No patience for suffering fools gladly or otherwise. Years and years later I would glance at myself in the mirror and see her face even though mine looked nothing like hers: my expressions, my reactions, the way my cheekbones cut into my eyes when I smiled. All of it Mother. Nature? Nurture? Both. Neither. Life had challenged and changed her, and it had done the same for me. How we each dealt with it was the only variant.

Mother never had a desire to change, none that we could see, anyway. No need to admit her failures, no desire, really, as far as I could see, to do anything other than what she had always done. Perhaps, had we gotten to Mother sooner, perhaps, had any of us been able to admit how bad the problem was, say, twenty years earlier, perhaps, had we not just dismissed her as a difficult, self-centered woman, perhaps, if we had been able to see beyond our own pain and into hers, we might have been able to save both Mother and ourselves. Or perhaps we would just have known about her illness sooner, and she would have spent more years in care.

But still we wondered whether or not, somewhere along the way, we might have convinced Mother that she was worth saving.

In the end, the diagnosis changed me. I became the daughter Mother always said she wanted: the easy, pleasing daughter who would, without too much bother, cater to her every whim. I slowly became even better at this role than Erika. I had more patience and was less invested. I had given away the future. The Biblical imperative to honor thy father and mother (and not ask too many questions) made sense to me now.

4.

I agreed to that week at the beach the second year because the memory of the first had almost faded, like the pain of birth dissipates enough for you to have another baby. Yet I was unsure enough about another week alone with her that I wanted a witness.

Paul and I tried so hard to keep Mother happy in the tiny house. But with another person there it was clear that the space that had been difficult enough for Mother and me the year before was impossible for three. The small portable television received only three stations; the radio received only public radio. Mother insisted on having one or the other on at all times. The noise drove Paul outside much of the week, where he sat reading in one of the plastic chairs on the lawn, moving the chair constantly to take advantage of the shade.

That second summer Mother seemed to take forever to get ready, even for a simple ride in the borrowed golf cart down to the shore for a beach walk: She could not find her sunglasses, her hat, her sneakers. She would wander the tiny house looking and looking as though she had a hundred rooms to search. Paul, more patient than I, reminded me that for this week we all had nothing *but* time. So I tried to wait, breathing slowly in and out, tried to sit back with a book of my own and just be. I knew from past experience that if I rushed Mother she would get upset and distracted and that any leave-taking would be stretched out beyond possibility.

While I cooked the evening meals in the hot kitchenette, Paul asked Mother questions and got her to tell stories, mostly about her past, her parents, her sisters. Back then there was nothing wrong with her memories of the past, it was only the previous week or day or hour she couldn't recall. Soon it would be a minute, a second. Then even that was gone. Although the stories were new to Paul at first, by the end of the week he had heard them many times. Still he listened attentively and warmly. I loved him for that.

He accompanied the two of us to the beach every day, even though he didn't love the sun and we had no umbrella for protection. Paul would hold Mother's arm as she walked down the rocky, somewhat treacherous path to the golf cart, something Mother would not allow me to do. She shook my arm off hers and said: "I'm *fine*." Yet, despite her illness, Mother retained vestiges of her expert flirtatiousness and Paul was just the kind of man she had always liked: He was handsome and smart and had old-fashioned, courtly manners that were respectful without being condescending. She was happy to have him help her.

Mother, although complimentary and grateful for my

dinners, protested each night that I served her too much food and Paul, always the gentleman, finished Mother's leftovers and refused to let her wash the dishes until I insisted. "Let her," I said. "It makes her happy to do something." Mother did seem content as she leaned over the tiny sink, soaping the dishes and pots and pans by hand, putting them in the strainer. She could stretch the task out to an hour.

Several nights, after supper, the three of us took the golf cart down to the shack on the boat dock for an ice cream. Mother was much more unsteady on her feet than she had been the summer before; she tired more easily after walking even short distances. I sensed it was partly depression at her illness (she still took medication for her moods), more than just physical infirmity, but while I would have relished the exercise, I drove Mother down the hill each evening and took a walk alone when Mother napped, which she did for a short while every afternoon. Paul insisted on staying behind in case Mother woke up.

One night that second summer, Paul, Mother and I headed up to Erika's house for dinner. Erika and her husband, Peter, had lived on the island for fifteen years and had a home with a breathtaking view of the sea. Mother hadn't been to Erika's since the summer of her diagnosis when I had slowly walked her up the hill only to have Erika refuse her wine.

For too many years, Mother's visits to Erika's, like those to the homes of all of her daughters, invariably ended in an argument with Mother threatening to leave, Mother drunk and angry, feeling neglected and put-upon, pulling a tantrum, making a fuss. Yelling. Leaving the room. Since the diagnosis, Erika had been worried, cautious, anxious about having Mother up to her house. She preferred to go off island and drive the hour and a half to Mother and take her out to lunch, spend a circumscribed amount of time that Erika felt she could control. Because Mother's relationship with all of us had been fractious and painful, even as the diagnosis turned a virago whose visits we anticipated with equal parts dread and fear into a dependent, tearful, frightened wreck, there was still enough history to make all of us fearful Old Mother might be waiting inside New Mother, ready, like a coiled snake, to strike. Her silence was unnerving. Mother had always been so loud before.

At dinner, as she had the summer before, Erika refused to serve wine with the meal, announcing, falsely: "We don't drink wine during the week." Even in her altered state, Mother, furious, knew Erika was lying. Her face set into a hard mask. But it wasn't as if she actually needed a drink. It wouldn't even have been the first drink of the day. Once again, as I had the summer before, I stocked the beach house with wine and daily soothed Mother with a before-dinner drink, a with-dinner drink, and an after-dinner drink. Or two. Or three. She'd had two glasses of wine before we even got to Erika's.

I took Erika into the kitchen and told her the truth and admonished her for trying to enforce her will on an old woman with whom it was impossible even to have a logical conversation. I told Erika that if I was taking care of Mother for a week, I would make it as easy on myself as possible. Cramped into a tiny beach house with a fishwife in withdrawal was not an option for me. But Erika could not be swayed.

"She should take pleasure in just being with us!" Erika said to me. She was near tears. "She should be happy with her daughters and her grandson and the beautiful view. Why does she need to drink?"

That was the eternal question. I couldn't believe that Erika was still asking it.

"I think," I said, slowly, patiently, "that perhaps if I had gotten the news she had, I'd drink, too. What's the point of staying sober when your future is already gone?" I felt this sincerely, even as I hated to see Mother drunk—it brought up terrible memories. But what would I have done had I gotten such a diagnosis? Would I have succumbed to a quick suicide or a slow one? Would I have fought and fought against the dark night creeping into my brain? Or would I have just succumbed to the inevitability of it? Would I have suddenly become a drunk or a drug addict? How long was the moment in which to make a choice? I didn't wish to think too hard about it.

I read an article in *The New York Times* wherein the author argued that our fear of forgetting was "irrational," I was infuriated. That we should just embrace the loss of memory inherent in aging, even if it should turn out to be the dreaded

A. That even those with that most heinous of diagnoses could have a meaningful life in the years that were left. I could not have disagreed more. If the bits of our memories that ebb with the tide of time are nothing like the Mack truck that has been driven through the brain of an Alzheimer's patient, any loss of memory has to invoke the dread of a potential complete loss. Ask the patient hurtling down the highway before the crash whether they would choose to wreck or hope for rescue: The answer is obvious. Are we really supposed to think that losing one's mind can be a good thing? *The Times* article writer argued that much mental and emotional ability can survive mere memory loss, but so far, I had seen no evidence of that. Looking at Mother, I saw little that was left of anything I recognized. Even her outer shell had begun to show the ravages of what was happening to her mind.

I could sit and talk with Mother for hours. I could and I did. But the conversation was one sided and meaningless. She would ask, "How are you doing?" I would reply with a different answer each time so I would not bore myself to death or break down into tears. I could not believe that what happened to her was a desirable thing in any way. The illness had softened her, yes, which was good, but at what price? And Mother had never made the conscious choice to soften her own *self*. She never would have. Why was a personality change foisted upon her by a destructive and devastating disease any kind of good thing?

Later that week, I lay with Paul in the small double bed we were sharing. Although this was the room Mother had the first year, she seemed happy enough to relinquish it and use the other bedroom with its twin beds, one to sleep in and one for a sort of closet, piled high with more than enough clothes for two or three weeks, without argument.

"She's worse than last year, much worse," I whispered to Paul. "You wouldn't know, of course, but she can't walk as far, she complains about not feeling well all the time, and her memory is going so fast it frightens me."

Paul got up on his elbow and turned toward me. "I'm sorry," he said. "I know it's hard on you, but I think she's having a good time. Even if all she says most of the time is 'gorgeous' or 'glorious.'"

I had to laugh. "At least it's a positive comment," I said. "And it is glorious here, isn't it?"

Paul kissed me on the forehead. "I am not nearly as enamored of this place as you and your sisters are," he said. "It's a little quiet for me. But since you're doing this for your mother, I am happy to be here with you."

It occurred to me that bringing Paul had been a mistake. I thought he would provide a welcome distraction, solace, a strong, warm body that could blot out my despair. But it had, in the end, been much easier that first year when I was alone with Mother. Tending to two people's widely opposite needs wasn't much fun. And Paul, as sweet as he was, clearly needed me to pay him attention. Despite everything. So, I

SHIVAH

lied. Yes, I lied. I said: "I'm so glad you are here, too."

5.

When she got out of Sanderstone the first time, Mother rented an apartment and moved her things from Tennessee to Rhode Island. She got a job. She managed. She seemed cured. She seemed who she had once been, at the least. But then, thirty years later, I saw she had written this in her journal:

> *After they had extinguished every sign of my existence, they began giving it back to me in little pieces, identifying marks in adhesive tape were pressed onto my razor, my body lotion, shampoo, tweezers, compact. My name, in blurred ink.*
>
> *I could not, now, gouge out my eyes or puncture my wrists with my rattail comb or overdose on lotion and astringent on the spur of a moment. I would have to plan, decide,*

go to the desk, give my name, retrieve my weapons, all before I could destroy or mutilate myself. If I wanted to die, would I have endured the last six months? Taken their pills, exposed my soul, and finally humiliated, shamed and dry-eyed, signed myself into this place?

I remembered an awful lunch one time when my bubbe and I had taken her out, near the end of her time there. I saw the three of us, Bubbe tearing her tissue again, Mother pushing an omelet around on her plate, tears welling up in her eyes. My bubbe, trying, as always, no matter what horrible thing had happened, to be cheerful and upbeat. My mother, huddled inside herself. It was a scene that would be repeated over and over and over every time I had a meal with Mother in *Menuchat Lev* or out at a restaurant. She would pretend to eat but really she pushed her food around the plate. She would ask me when I was leaving and then her eyes would fill and she would tell me she would miss me. Even if I had just arrived.

Had I read her words earlier, I might have understood more. Or better, I might have seen that she was still extraordinarily fragile and that little about our relationship would change, despite her life-altering surrender. And so, much, much later, when Mother forgot even how to write her own name, forgot who she had been, who she was, after she lost nearly everything, I thought back on that passage and how she was even less than the blurred ink that had identified her when she wrote about her nervous breakdown and her first time in Sanderstone.

6.

"Our normal waking consciousness is but one special type of consciousness whilst all about it, parted from it by the flimsiest of screens, there lie potential forms of consciousness entirely different." —William James

I have always lived on at least two plains: the real and the supernatural, the actual and that built on faith and, yes, superstition. My fear and superstition travelled as far as the generations I knew about, the poor, uneducated peasants who took the boat from Russia to Ellis Island. From bubbes on both sides I learned the rituals: spitting at the evil eye, knocking on wood, keeping the devil at bay. Although I am a rational woman most of the time, I believe in evil and I suspect it believes in me. There is too much unknowable about our world. Too much we can't explain. Too much that makes no sense.

Parents should love their children but some, too many, don't. Children should adore their parents, but often that is impossible. There is horror, inexplicable depravity, tragedy, all around us. If good exists in the world, and it does, then its converse must also be true.

I needed the faith to make it possible to even imagine a life no longer under my mother's thumb. Mother would have laughed if she heard me speak of any influence she had over me. But I spent a lifetime trying not to be like her. Trying to make my own way out of my heredity seemed like a lifelong process. A role model can tell you what to avoid as well as what to emulate. I was beginning to feel very brittle. Soon, I would be an orphan for real, instead of just metaphorically. Sooner than I would like to think about, I will leave my own child orphaned. But I keep knocking wood and spitting just to be safe.

With Mother's diagnosis grew a larger, more intense and unhinged faith in me that there is something larger than any of us. Science but more than that. The original belief in God was born out of violence and disbelief. I can believe in Him and admit He is unknown. I can admit that He may not exist at all. Like Mother's memories He could be locked away somewhere, a kidnap victim living in a narrow room and waiting for rescue. When I think about God, I feel like a detective searching for a missing person. Occasionally I think I spot Him, but He is just beyond my reach;

SHIVAH

He turns a corner and disappears.

What matters most in my belief is actually the final acceptance that most things, maybe all things, are beyond my control. Most things are beyond my knowing, too. But they are just about all beyond my control. I have never really wanted a life that was completely knowable and therefore controllable and therefore absolutely predictable—I don't think most people want that. But still, I have spent so much of my life trying very hard to know: searching for meaning, for love, for purpose.

All of us cling to what comforts us, what makes it possible, even desirable, for us to get up in the morning, even if our very existence is based only on the most basic of our belief systems. No matter how nonsensical those belief systems are, the only thing that counters them is our desire for something else. But when reality and desire bump up against each other it is not a Venn diagram: Reality pushes desire completely out of the picture. Knowing replaces not knowing and not knowing replaces knowing. We go about our days as though we and life make perfect sense when nothing makes sense at all. I wonder, too, what must Alzheimer's feel like as it runs its course: To know and not to know, to know and not to know why, and then finally to not know at all?

7.

I tried many times, alone and with my sisters, to wash my hands of Mother. I had banished her from my life, vanquished her from my dreams. I had stepped far back from her, set up new rules of the road. But when I got the news of the diagnosis, when I saw Mother give in to that diagnosis so quickly, as though she were both expecting and dreading it, the mother who had abandoned us came home: It was as if the missing mother of Cinderella or Snow White had suddenly risen from the dead.

In those classic fairy tales full of dead mothers and the abandoned children who long for rescue by fate or fairy godmother or handsome prince, the child endures the abandonment. Abandoned children have to rise to their own resilience, make up their own minds whether they will succumb to victimization or pull themselves up by the bootstraps and make that seven-league journey alone. But none of the kids in the fairy tales have to deal with the lost mother returning. The lost mother needing them to step up. The lost mother no longer simply metaphorically lost, now there in her body, yet still lost forever.

As a child I loved playing what I named The Orphan Game. I made myself into a foundling who had somehow ended up in the wrong house. I was completely convinced that Mother was not my real mother, that Father was not my real father; I had been mixed up at the hospital and given to the wrong family. Perhaps I hadn't been technically an orphan, but I had no idea whether my real parents were dead or alive: all I was sure of was that they were not the people in whose house I lived.

Like many lonely children, I was sure I had been abandoned on the doorstep of the wrong house. Along with my vivid and often macabre imagination (I imagined myself poor, lost, motherless, dying of a heroic disease), I was also a voracious reader and identified strongly with heroines who were in the wrong place at the wrong time: I easily found a kind of alternative real life in the books I devoured. I separated myself from the life that Mother had created for me, my sisters, my father by reading the biographies of Jane Addams and Clara Barton and Florence Nightingale and Sacagawea—women who had overcome difficulties far greater than mine. Women who suffered traumas much greater than neglect or indifference. Or moodiness. I wanted to be them and not me.

I was fascinated by tragedy and idolized Johnny

Tremain whose hand was scarred by molten silver. I liked always to imagine myself a player in a life of great and overwhelming tragedy. But I also imagined myself coming through it all stronger and more able. Even books like *The Count of Monte Cristo* and *Les Misérables* fascinated the precocious me who wanted nothing more than some huge injustice to fight against. A merely miserable family was not quite dramatic enough.

Sara Crewe was an early role model; I read a thin, abridged Scholastic paperback edition for the first time when I was eight years old, and then I read it over and over until it was nearly worn through. A couple of years later, I graduated to the full version. I loved the story of the misbegotten little princess. I knew her as surely as if she lived next door. I wanted to be her, even in her deprivation and loneliness. I envied how her goodness radiated despite the cruelty she was subjected to. I was enthralled by the fantasies of a better life that slipped into her garret. I thought someone would rescue me, too, if I just waited long enough and was good enough and stoic enough. Sara remained sunny. I would too. I was so convinced of my rescue that I left my bedroom window open ready to receive my own little monkey bearing gifts and the chance of a new life. The unsettling part was that while I felt I lived in a cottage with a witch who would just as soon eat me as anything, all of my friends, like Paul, believed instead that I was a princess in a castle. The house was large and beautiful, Mother was larger than life and beautiful. A superb actress, she often even convinced us, her own children, that it was we who saw the world skewed. That our vision of reality was foolish and silly. She wasn't going to cook us and eat us!

Even years down the road Mother would change the story of our early years at will, admonishing us for recalling things that simply could not have been true. We had no way of knowing, even as we moved into our twenties, just how sick my mother was, and just how powerful was the disease that led to her own self-deception.

My best friend Pam loved to come to my house because compared to her own it seemed so very normal. Our house was big and decorated and modern and airy: I had my own room. Pam had to share a small bedroom with her aging grandmother. My parents seemed to love each other while her mother and stepfather played a passive-aggressive game that both of us, even as children, understood was dangerous. Pam's stepfather was an alcoholic abuser and although her mother was kind and lovely, she allowed Pam to live in terror and pain because she simply could not manage to leave. Even when Pam came to live with me for the last year of high school and saw firsthand the everyday insanity of life with Mother, still she thought it far superior to her own.

"Your mother saved my life. That matters," Pam has said. More than once. And, yes, it was absolutely true. When Pam's mother and stepfather decided to move to the Midwest right in the middle of high school, Pam, in protest at leaving me, her other friends, her familiar life, resolved to starve herself. Thanksgiving weekend, a few months after their move, I talked Mother into a plane ticket to visit Pam and what I saw both frightened and impressed me. I admitted a kind of envy: Pam was completely in control of her own life, and her protest, if sad, was also somehow beautiful. Pam's mother seemed oblivious to the fact that Pam was vanishing before her very eyes, but I returned home and, dramatic as my mother ever was, said: "*We have to save her!*"

Like me, Mother could often be counted on to be superior in a big crisis, if necessary. It was just the everyday stuff that confounded her. Once, during freshman year of college, sick with despair at keeping up with the private school educated kids who far outpaced me in education and experience, I called my parents to tell them I was dropping out. My father laughed and hung up the phone, but in a very rare moment of insight and generosity, Mother wrangled the New York City flat of an old friend and sent me off for a week's respite. I needed a break. Mother understood breaks. She might have done well as a battlefield nurse, tending to crisis after crisis. But she was a housewife with three daughters who lived in a small Southern town, and she couldn't begin to manufacture enough real, important crises to keep her occupied. So, when something came along that used up her relentless energy, she jumped in with both feet; the ordinary despair of life was not enough to make her feel necessary and happy.

Mother, rising to the occasion of everyone's tragedy but her own, didn't even argue. Back then, we had no words for what Pam had but Mother believed me when I showed her a photo of Pam. She called Pam's mother and laid out the plan. She would not take no for an answer: Pam would live with us until she was out of high school.

At dinner the first night of Pam's new life, Mother said simply, "You must eat something."

And Pam said, "I will have an apple."

My mother put one at Pam's place. The next day she went to the market and bought a huge bag of the best apples she could find and laid them by Pam's place each evening. Pam ate them, one by one, two by two, and she was well again. It was that simple.

I know that today girls are hospitalized and often fed intravenously against their will; I saw it happen to one of Ivy's schoolmates. I know that many girls never recover. I know about Karen Carpenter and the models who have starved themselves right out of life. But those girls never knew my mother. They never had her offer them one shiny red apple.

8.

There was something so counter-intuitive about returning to Mother again, full force like we did, after her diagnosis. Something weird and unsettling about trying to be the daughters we should have been, the daughters she wanted us to be, after we tried too hard for so many years to extricate our lives from hers, to break free of the strings that attached us to the puppet master. The ways in which she treated us over the years could still be resurrected from memory with little effort, no matter how hard we all pressed to keep them hidden. We allowed ourselves to admit that coming back to stand at her side was like the advice to steer into a skid. It sounded wrong

I wonder: Are the children whose mothers are with them in flesh but not spirit, who feel abandoned not physically like in a fairy tale but emotionally, psychically, are *they* able to be rescued? There are no dwarves to give them a safehouse, no prince to awaken them with a kiss. No one is coming up fast on a white stallion to save them. What is to be made of them? What do they become?

Dead mothers, abandoned children: The stuff of fairy tales. It is no wonder no one writes tales like that anymore. It is obvious that were anyone brave enough to do so, writers would have to be ironic. No one can take that sort of stuff seriously: It is too common. Children die of neglect every day. Neglect, abandonment, misguided love. And even so, we are all supposed to just pick ourselves up and go on, despite everything. We are not allowed to remain victims. It is weak and unproductive. I actually agree with that. I rescued myself by sheer force of will.

But if the fairy tales I gobbled up so voraciously in my youth included pages of caveats and, perhaps, a self-help section in the back—notes, say, on how to tell poison apples from real ones—might I have been able to make my escape a lot sooner? I have been told by my father that when he took me to see Snow White at three years old, I jumped up and yelled, "Snow White, don't eat that apple!" and after she did, I said loudly, "I told you so!" Was I always interested in wise self-preservation, in warnings? Like those ads for Charles Atlas or Sea-Monkeys in the back of comic books, wouldn't we all have benefited from a coupon in the back of Grimm's that offered a discount on motivational tapes: "A Fairy Godmother Tells You How You Can Overcome Being Abandoned and Get Back on Track." Perhaps, in my case, the cautions may not have worked. My mother could rescue a child like Pam with an apple while completely ignoring the hunger of her own children.

Really, kids are mostly on their own, anyway, all save the truly lucky ones. Watch the news, read the papers: You can send money, send food, send medicine, but in the end, what saves a person is ineffable.

My sisters and I had just winged it, no instructions extant. And we were still flying by the seat of our pants. Many years ago, Sara showed me a poem she had written. Inspired by the insane headlines of supermarket tabloids, it was entitled, "Duck Rescues Boy from Drowning."

> *I was rescued many times from drowning*
> *As a child, by animals of every kind,*
> *every shape. Black Beauty picked me*
> *out of deep despair a hundred times,*
> *Beautiful Joe, King of the Wind*
> *helped salvage me. Abused, abandoned, they*
> *were rescued and lived happy lives, it could*
> *happen. They found My Lady wandering in*
> *a swamp, took that dog home and loved*
> *her till her father, the real father, came*
> *to claim her. Paddington was picked up*
> *in a station luggage room. His tag read take*
> *care of this bear, and someone did. The horse*
> *said love could make a velvet rabbit live.*

I didn't need to read that poem to know how Sara felt.

I thought about a movie I saw in which a character, catching a family member reading *The Velveteen Rabbit* said: "Heavy stuff." Heavy stuff indeed. But who really knows what care or love *could* do? It could save lives, but couldn't it destroy them, too? Isn't love dangerous if it cripples the person who is loved? If love is given with the expectation of its return in equal force, isn't it a selfish, absorbing, damning love? Unconditional love never seemed on the menu at our house. Mother's inability to mother always escaped her ability to recognize that inability existed at all.

The Dunning-Kruger Effect has been all the rage when talking about politics in the twenty-first century, but long before our current crop of villainous politicians, I saw firsthand that incompetence masks our ability to *recognize* our own incompetence. *Anosognosia:* the condition in which a person who suffers from a disability seems unaware of or denies the existence of the disability. Mother was like that. Despite the evidence, despite her own mental illness, she remained convinced that she had been a wonderful mother. Flawed, perhaps, but no more so than anyone else.

9.

A month after Mother's diagnosis, when she was still in the holding pattern before finally landing at *Menuchat Lev*, I met Erika at Mother's house for the initial cleanup before the home went on the market. I wasn't sure quite what to expect, Mother had been so good at hiding the detritus of her life from us. I suppose I suspected chaos but nothing prepared me for the reality of it. I parked out front, noticed the garden was full of weeds, and opened the door onto Erika standing in the middle of the kitchen, nearly in tears.

When Erika said, "It's worse than it looks," I burst out laughing.

"It *can't* be worse than it looks," I said. "It looks horrifying."

"I think I meant to say it's not as bad as it looks," Erika laughed.

"But then you would also be wrong. Because it *is* as bad as it looks."

Erika agreed. She had been here for two hours already

and half-filled green garbage bags littered the rooms. And I, the kind of woman who would hugely, loudly, shout *fuck fuck fuck fuck fuck* if I dropped a pan on my toe, who found interstate traffic completely debilitating, who could easily lose her temper when her daughter spilled or broke something, who came apart at Hallmark commercials and terrible Lifetime Network movies, whose emotions were often on the surface, well, that woman just wasn't in the house. I suddenly recognized a kinship to my mother, however frightening. Huge crises did not undo me; they made me stronger. I did not come apart at the thought of cleaning out nearly thirty years of junk. I did not dissolve into tears. I did not yell. My heart did not beat wildly in my chest. I simply stood surveying the disaster that sat in the center of the living room. And I took a deep breath.

"You're so calm," Erika said.

"What choice do I have?" Like Mother I was good in a real tragedy: My ability to cope took over my despair. Huge things, large scary things did not faze me nearly as much as the insanity of everyday life. And I knew, as I said it, that we really did not have a choice. This was something we were meant to do because we *could*.

Choice. Another conundrum. Do we have it or do we not? Does the randomness of the universe mean that all our choices are equal or that they are all meaningless? I have long struggled with the notion that if responses to things are hardwired into the brain, free will might not exist at all. The notion that there are choices to be made is just another thing, like putting on the same shoes before every interview or wearing the same socks to every game during a championship, that makes you *feel* in control. But it's only a feeling.

A few years ago, I had an odd and comforting moment while listening to Ivy make her way through yet another awful piece of music at yet another piano recital. I suddenly no longer believed that my daughter's performance was a reflection of me. For years, I had held my breath whenever she performed, whenever she was called on to do something in front of others. And I noticed lots of other parents doing it then, visibly holding their breaths, clenching their fists, leaning forward when their child went up to play. Couples would grab each other's hand, not out of affection and pride, but as a sort of a prayer: *Please let him get through the song without a stumble.* But there I was, that afternoon, suddenly calm, just listening to Ivy play. If she made a mistake, so be it. I could no longer invest my energy in whether or not someone played better than her; if she did well, the praise would come; if she failed to play beautifully, Ivy would have to accept the disappointment. Nothing I could do while I sat and listened to her would make a difference. I hadn't exactly been a helicopter mother like you read about in the news, but I had tried to be exactly the opposite of my mother. I was *involved.* Perhaps too much so. And at some moment I had to learn to let go. Ivy at ten years old playing the piano was my time. My time to start the process. Children have to own their mistakes as well as their successes. I have not perfected this philosophy, but I have alleviated some of the Sturm und Drang that is childrearing. I knew I would always love Ivy unequivocally, but I couldn't be invested in her as someone who propped up my own self-image.

There had been no such break between Mother and her daughters, no natural, easy one, anyway. Mother so clearly still held her breath, so keenly still clenched her fists at every moment her daughters might make her proud or embarrassed. When I was newly married to my first husband, she came for a visit and I, ill-advisedly, showed her the latest short story I had written. She read it and then looked at me solemnly and said: "I suppose you should get used to this being as good as you're ever going to get." I couldn't move for a moment. But I wasn't going to cry or even speak to her about it. Instead, I picked up the manuscript and took it with me and never showed her anything I wrote again. When things began to be published nationally, I kept them from her.

The irony was that the person most responsible for our slipups was Mother. There was no way we could either live up to or down to her expectations of us. Each day was a new adventure: She would send us out into the world, reeling with expectations or crushed by defeat. Any investment in what Mother felt about us was our own cudgel.

Both Mother and Father were pretty much completely disinterested in anything we children did unless it directly impacted them.

It was during my younger years that I began to think about God. I didn't pray to Him for anything as I pretty much understood that was useless. I did try and speak with Him, however, even conscious as I was that He had left me and my sisters to our own devices. And it wasn't that we were beaten or starved—I knew children in school who were both—it was just that we were pretty much ignored, or, on the opposite end, yelled at. It was only later as an adult that I began to be grateful that I had survived, that I was strong and resilient and that I had even flourished. I never expected punishment, and I never expected miracles. It was, oddly enough, that life-long silence that brought me back to Him. That and tempting fate by having a child. I understood that God does not dole out favors, He does not act arbitrarily; He is simply another choice we humans make. I saw Him as familiar, someone who suffered from His own odd kind of manic depression. First He created, then He destroyed. First He was insistent on obeisance and then He disappeared.

Jack Miles says in his "biography" of God that, "A deeper knowledge of God can serve to render conscious and sophisticated what is otherwise typically unconscious and naïve." He goes on to posit that we Westerners search for the simple but actually revere the complex. I think we are suspicious of the simple. We think it's easy. And therefore meaningless. We are meant to suffer.

And if one believes in that suffering, if one believes that there is no easier way to be human, it is easy to see why

Mother held so tight to her unhappiness, reveled in an illness she wouldn't name or even admit to having. She relished in the awful days because she would not willingly give up her glorious days. Like so many people with bipolar disorder, she *needed* to feel those huge highs to counter the deep lows: An existence on one plane would not do. The pain and the joy were both necessary to keep her alive, even as they broke her, too. Mother never understood that the alcohol mediated her life in such a way that when it was gone so, too, was her mind. Unlike our bipolar God, Mother did not have an infinite existence in which to travel from thunder to silence. Her time had been short and it was now, effectively, up.

"You're right," Erika said as we surveyed all the work we would have to do to empty Mother's house. "We have no choice. None at all."

"Actually"—I walked over to hug her—"we *do* have a choice. There is always a choice. We need to remember that. At least immediately and minimally. For instance, we could *not* do it. We could hire someone."

"We couldn't do that." Erika was aghast. She didn't want to have a sense of duty, but she did, as did all of us.

"No, *we* probably couldn't," I admitted. We were still too caught up in Mother's vortex. We were still processing her diagnosis and what it would mean. "But we could. *If we could*," I said. "It's just that we can't."

We understood our own faulty logic, and for five incredibly long days we cleaned the house of more than twenty-five years of newspapers, magazines, old letters, typed journal entries, bits and bobs of short stories and novels begun and abandoned (the only completed works were from her time in New York City in her twenties), receipts for things that we could find no evidence of, and piles and piles of manila envelopes stuffed with clippings: *Things to read someday* scribbled on the outside. Of *every one*. That "someday" had come and gone so long ago. We assumed they were more of the ephemera Mother began sending all of us when we left home: articles and magazine pieces she thought would interest us tucked in with the letters she sent us. On the top of each was scribbled: *Thought you should know about this. Isn't this fascinating!* Or *Did you know this?* As we and Mother grew older the scraps of newsprint would often come without a letter as if the article illustrated all that Mother had to offer. Erika filled a huge plastic bag with manila envelope after manila envelope. She cried, "I thought she had sent us everything. But look! A treasure trove of things unsent."

Into thirty huge black garbage bags nearly thirty years of papers went.

On the second day of cleaning Mother's house, I sat on the back porch, smoking a cigarette, dropping the ash into Mother's large pot of dead begonias. It was a decently warm early New England summer, and I leaned back in one of Mother's matching wooden Adirondack chairs and closed my eyes for a moment. I remembered all the many times—since Mother had come back north, gotten out of the hospital after her breakdown and bought the house—that I alone, and then my ex-husband Ben and I, and then Ben and Ivy and I, had driven down this street. I remembered that every time, at the moment I spied the tiny, painted house, fear and anticipation and dread and desire captured my heart. The visits made alone were the hardest: Mother waiting at the door for me with a glass of wine in hand to give me as soon as I walked in.

For years she needed, *wanted*, complicity in her drinking. I hesitated, always, between my own need to calm my hands, my heart and my "virtuous" desire not to give in to her hardened belief that the wine was a mere social nicety. I would sip my glass, trying to make it last. Mother would finish the large bottle.

I opened my eyes and could see my mother proudly weeding the garden surrounding me, a garden that had contained only purple, dark pink and white flowers. A riotous, untidy English garden that was also very beautiful. But in the few weeks since her absence, the gardens had already become heavy with weeds. I heard a voice, hesitant but close by.

"I'm Barry . . . from across the street?"

I got up. "Oh, hi."

"I saw all the cars and, well, I just wondered what was going on." He took in the mound of plastic garbage bags. "You're one of her daughters, right? We met once."

I remembered him. Barry and Don lived across the

street, a couple with whom Mother exchanged house watching duties while she, or they, were on vacation. Occasionally Mother had called to tell me she was looking after Snowball, Barry and Don's huge, overstuffed Persian cat, for a few days.

"Yeah, I'm Leah," I said. "You're the guy with the cat."

Barry laughed. "She loves that cat, although she pretends she doesn't."

I suspected that Mother really *didn't* love the cat at all but felt virtuous taking care of it. Each time she babysat Snowball, she called one of us to let us know she was taking care of a cat. As if it were an elephant. Or a tiger. Or a dodo bird.

"Sit down?" I asked.

Barry sat tentatively on the edge of a bench. "Is something wrong?"

"We're selling the house. Mom can't live here anymore. She has Alzheimer's. We just got the diagnosis." Saying it out loud to a stranger was weird. But I found it easier than I would have thought to say the words out loud. I rushed on: "She can't be alone. She can't take care of herself, can't drive. Erika and I are cleaning out the house so we can put it on the market."

Barry didn't look too surprised. "She's been keeping to herself a lot lately," he said. "I wondered if something was wrong. We went away for a week to the Cape and asked her if she could look after Snowball and, for the first time, she seemed a little scared by our request. She hesitated and then she said she didn't think she could handle it. I told Don I thought something was going on."

He got up. "I'm sorry," he said. "Is there anything I can do? Do you and Erika need something to eat?"

"No," I said. "Thanks. Erika's gone off to get us sandwiches or something. We're fine."

"Where will your mother go?"

"We're trying to get her into that new residential living place, *Menuchat Lev*. It may be a few weeks. We don't know if they have any room. But my uncle has some pull."

"Will you let us know? If I come over with my telephone number, will you call us and let us know? We'd like to visit."

"Sure," I said. "That would be nice. She'd appreciate it, I'm sure."

Barry went to shake my hand and then, on second thought, leaned into me for an awkward hug. "I'm really sorry," he said. I said I was sorry, too.

So this is how it goes, I thought, sitting back down. Then, needing to keep the momentum going, I got up and walked around to the front of the house to get another pack of cigarettes from my car. So this is how it goes. The refrain to a Tori Amos song came into my head: "When I come to terms, to terms with this, my world will change for me."

As I leaned back out of the car seat, I noticed that Mother's next-door neighbor was painting his house. He bought it just a few months before, from Mother's long-time neighbor who had gone into a nursing home.

"I like that color," I said, slamming the car door and

walking to the edge of the two lots.

"Do you? I do, too." The man stepped back and surveyed the pale dove grey that was replacing the worn white on the clapboards. "We're not sure what to do about the trim. We thought, perhaps, a darker blue-grey."

"That would work," I said. "Just don't *ongepotchket* it up."

The man laughed. "I haven't heard that word since my grandmother died." He walked over and held out his hand and said, "I'm Richard. I'm a doctor. I know about your mom. I'm sorry."

Suddenly I felt like just sitting down and weeping. For the first time it hit me in my heart. If Erika did not get back with the sandwiches quickly . . .

He looked at me carefully. He read my mind. He spoke my fears. "Don't worry," he said, "by the time you or your sisters have to worry about this disease, they'll have a cure, a vaccine even. I'm sure of it."

Each of us was more afraid of it happening to one of the others than to ourselves. *Nisht do gedachet*. And each of us tried to decide how we would handle it should we get a diagnosis like Mother's. We wondered: Would we want to know? How soon would we want to know, if at all? The incurable nature of the disease, coupled with the fact that at any point in it we would not even remember we had it, confounded us. I thought Mother's neighbor was being very kind and extremely optimistic. There would be no vaccine. At least not in my lifetime.

Still, I scoured the internet and whenever I saw something pertinent, I passed it along to Erika and Sara. Anything about new research caught my eye as I wondered what was reasonable to believe and what seemed a pipe dream. I refused to believe the best because all I had seen was the worst. New research stated that the disease starts showing up even earlier than was previously expected; people as young as I was had fallen ill. Bubbe had begun to seriously deteriorate in her late seventies but lived another thirteen years; Mother's was found when she was seventy-eight, but it was clear that she had been suffering its effects for at least a few years, try as she had to keep herself together.

"From your mouth to God's ears," I said, not believing him for a moment, and grateful to hear a car come down the street: Erika, back at last.

How the hell did he know that was what was worrying me most, I wondered? How could he see through to my selfishness, to the core of my worry? How did he know that I could trace a line from my bubbe to Mother to myself without even being really conscious of it? How did he know that all the bits and pieces that had slipped away from the past two generations were just waiting to slip away from me? That the still eager, still growing (I hoped) mind I had was hobbled by the fear of losing it and not knowing about it until it was too late to do anything about it? For the past few weeks it had all but paralyzed me, late at night, as I lay in bed. Did it show, my fear, my anxiety, my helplessness? Was it that obvious? Despite the fact that I behaved normally, spoke in rational sentences and was still in possession of my faculties, was there already some fraying of the edges that was obvious to everyone but me?

What separates the ordinary, normal act of forgetting from the seeds that will blossom into the complete loss of memory? And if, as doctors believe, the signs, the changes begin in midlife or even earlier, how do we monitor them without giving over our present to a preservation of both the past and the future? The doctor next door to my mother may have been right, but nothing in the literature I have read indicates real progress, except perhaps the earlier diagnosis of a disease already ravaging the insides of our brain, except perhaps the treatment that may arrest the freefall for a tiny amount of time. Even if genetic markers can indicate a tendency to Alzheimer's—in fact, it's a fifty-fifty chance that offspring will have the same markers—less than one percent of Alzheimer's patients have those markers. It's all a crapshoot.

One doctor I discovered said there is a very long phase when people are not themselves. But what about Mother? Which Mother was it who was not her *self*? The very cruel one had already pretty much disappeared, or at least her barbs were now dull. The Mother who thought our every move was out to get her, that one was gone, too. The tough Mother who lived alone even with a broken foot, which meant she'd had to go up and down her tiny wooden stairs on her bottom, she was definitely gone. How could I recognize the Mother who remained?

I told Erika about both visits from the neighbors as we ate our lunch. And then I broached the subject we had all been afraid to touch.

"The doctor next door said that by the time we get it, if we do get it, they'll have a cure. I would love to believe him, but I can't."

Erika shook her head. "I don't want to talk about that. Besides we're already old. We could already have it."

"Yes," I said, "that is the point. We *are* already well into middle age. The plaques and tangles in our brain could just be waiting to strike. Don't you forget things? Where you're going, where the keys are, what day it is?"

"I daily walk into a room and forget what I went there for," I said. "But until now I always assumed it was because I'm so preoccupied. The same reason I walk into tables and trip on the sidewalk when there's nothing there."

"It's more than that," Erika said. "We do have a history, and we could. But I can't think about it. Not now, anyway."

I gave up. When Erika pronounced a subject closed it was indeed closed.

We resumed our cleaning. In the drawer of a hutch that took up most of a tiny room off the kitchen, I found a huge box of candle ends and stubs. Purple, mostly, my mother's favorite color. I laughed when I thought about telling the neighbor not to overdo his paint job: Mother's house was the gaudiest on the street, painted as if it were a huge gingerbread Victorian instead of a small cottage. The siding was a deep mocha, the trim fuchsia, the stairs and shutters an unusual shade of purple. It worked in an odd way, but it had been hell for Mother to keep up. I wondered what new colors the house would be painted by its new owners. (When I drove curiously by the house a year after Mother moved out, I saw that the new owner hadn't touched a single color.)

As I pawed through Mother's candle "collection," I could not imagine what made her save them; some were barely an inch tall. There were dozens of stubs that wouldn't give off another half hours' worth of illuminations. Like the mounds of paper we had already gone through, the candles felt like they held a message that I couldn't read. Some secret we were not privy to.

Her affection for candles and low lighting was the stuff of legend: like Blanche DuBois, she knew she looked better in candlelight. When I would get out of my car after the long drive up north, come to the back door and step inside, the house was often so dim I could barely see to let go of my luggage—the lights on dimmers pushed way down, tiny mood lamps dotting the living room. And everywhere there would be candles, some sticks, some votives, some pillars, all flickering and throwing shadows.

In the earlier days, Mother would have a meal ready when Ben, Ivy and I came to visit. Nothing fancy. Nothing like dinners in the old days when I had been a child at home. But she might have a cold poached salmon, a salad, brownies from the corner bakery. Always, too, the sweating and already open liter of white wine. But for the half dozen years before she got sick, Mother began to order in and send me out to pick up. Finally, in the last two years before she was diagnosed—when she was clearly not quite herself—she would insist we all go out for dinner. "I have nothing in the house," she would say. "I haven't had time to go shopping. Let's go to one of the places on Hope Street." I might have wondered what she was doing all day, but it didn't seem right to start a fight. I now know she had simply stopped shopping, stopped even eating very much. All her resources, all she had left, she martialed for the two hours of the evening before the wine and the disease sent her to bed.

 I was actually rather relieved to walk up the street to a restaurant. I relished the chance to stretch my legs after hours of sitting in a car and the prospect of eating something faintly exotic that I could not find in the small town in Virginia where I lived was exciting. And I was always glad for an hour or two out of Mother's claustrophobic house. I had yet to discover the secrets it harbored: The years of neglect she hid behind closed doors. But the older she grew, the smaller her house seemed to be, too. How did none of us quite understand how far down the rabbit hole our Alice had fallen?

When Erika and I went into Mother's house to clean, Mother's refrigerator was nearly empty. The few bottles of condiments had crusted lids that looked like something from a school science project. The cupboard was full of cans years out of date, the drawers held spices that no longer gave off fragrance, those candle stubs, like the years old cans of foodstuffs, like the jars of spices that had long ago lost their smells, were just symbols of the decay that had long ago fully taken hold. I swept them all into yet another black plastic garbage bag.

At four o'clock each day—at just the moment when we began to fade both mentally and physically—Erika went to the mini mart down the road and bought each of us a can of diet Rock Star, an energy drink that I have not been able to drink since. We downed the cans and kept working. Clothes from twenty years past went into bags, some for Goodwill, some for the garbage. The clothes had been cheap to begin with—Mother was tight with money even when she didn't have to be. Although the clothes seemed clean there was a mustiness about them that tickled my nose and made me feel as though I was going through the things of a woman who was already dead. It wasn't just the particular smell of the elderly, it was the smell of death. I shuddered at the off-brand labels and remembered many an argument begun by Mother over some handbag or pair of shoes I would be wearing. "Oh, Leah," Mother would say in her trademark tone, somewhere between affected disinterest and clear disdain. "Is that *new*? It looks *expensive*. I could never afford *anything* like that." Mother talked in italics.

And if her vocabulary had become more limited, Mother could still speak in her trademark italics. The subject grew ever slimmer, the same expressions used over and over, but she always punctuated with a visibly slanted emphasis. That second summer at the beach house Mother had alternated between the single words *glorious*, or *gorgeous*, used alone or in the variant of a phrase. No matter what the descriptor—the view, dinner, an evening out—the same phrases would come out of her mouth: "*Isn't this* gorgeous?" "*Isn't* this *gorgeous?*" "*Gorgeous, just gorgeous.*" At one point, Paul admitted he might lose his mind.

"Well," I told him. "My bubbe, the last fifteen years of *her* life, said only, 'Isn't this lovely!' And Mother always *was* more than a tad hyperbolic."

After Erika and I got as much garbage and detritus and memories and other things out of Mother's house, Hannah arranged for it to be staged by her decorator, a man whose taste I didn't much care for—too froufrou for me—but who ultimately did a remarkable job. The house looked nothing like it had when Mother lived there. Gone was the whimsy, the charm, the chaos. It looked settled and clean, spare and much larger. The market was still good then and it sold within a week to a young, single schoolteacher for our full asking price.

For the first weeks at Rosewood, Mother's temporary living quarters after she was discharged from Sanderstone and before we got her a place at *Menuchat Lev*, Mother asked about the house, said she wished to go and see it one more time. She seemed aware that she could no longer live there, but I couldn't bear to even take her back for a visit. After it was cleaned and staged, it was unrecognizable. It would have been cruel and unusual punishment to walk her through the door. Better to let her remember it as she had decorated and lived in it, as it had been both sanctuary and prison: She had thought it a temporary residence but it was her last house if not her final home. Better to let her remember it however she could.

But for every time she accused us of selling her house out from under her, with the next breath she would begin to weep and thank us for all the work we had done. She would gesture around her apartment, thank us for how it was furnished, acknowledge how we had moved everything she really loved into *Menuchat Lev*. She would say, "I wish I'd had a chance to see my house one more time. I wish I could have made the decisions." But then she would say, "Oh, it must have been so difficult for you, to go through everything. It was a bit of a mess."

A bit of a mess. A bit of an understatement. None of us could have quite imagined the mountains of mess that Mother had hidden behind doors and closets and drawers. Amidst the trash, Erika and I found months of unopened bank statements, unpaid bills, bills paid twice or even three times, checks to charities to which Mother had donated half a dozen separate times in one year. It wasn't just the foodstuffs in the pantry that were years out of date. Mother's whole life had stopped sometime in the past and she had been stuck there for God only knew how long.

And even though Mother had still had a car and could drive, we discovered she hadn't done so in weeks, perhaps months, since getting lost on the way to the hairdresser who had been doing her hair for years. We had put all this disarray down to her increasing alcohol intake. But the truth was that somewhere, somehow, we all knew and we didn't know. Because we didn't want to know. Ida, my bubbe, had dementia for nearly twenty years before she died. Back then, no actual diagnosis of Alzheimer's was given. Mother's symptoms mimicked her own mother's exactly: the placidity, the giving up, the repetitions. So everyone knew. I knew. We all knew. Somewhere in the back of our minds, we must have known. The shock of the diagnosis was not the shock of the unknown, but the shock of having our worst fears realized.

For a while, like asking to go back to the house, Mother railed about her new situation, even if she railed as a somewhat kinder, gentler version of herself.

"What am I doing here?" she would say. "How long until I can go home?" And then, "I hate this place, there is nothing to do and everyone is old, old, old."

It was not at all true that at *Menuchat Lev* there was nothing to do: The place had a list of activities that made my head swim. Okay, it was true that the residents were old and most of them looked it. There were lots of men bent over canes or walkers, women in wheelchairs. It *was* true that everyone looked older than Mother, even I could see that. But as I kept reminding her: Appearances were deceiving. Mother may have looked young, but her mind was gone. Most of the other residents looked old and infirm, but they were still going on outings, visiting their children, playing games, reading the newspaper. Remembering.

10.

I understood from Mother's doctors and from the reading I had done, that the average life span of a person with Alzheimer's is eight to ten years. Six years on, Mother was still somewhat familiar. The unsteadiness of her gait that first year's trip to the beach had resolved itself. She seemed to have achieved some sort of stasis where she wasn't getting worse by leaps and bounds but we had no idea how long that would last. Alzheimer's, like cancer, seems to hit each person uniquely, and so we had no idea when any of this would end, or how, or even where. What we did know was that we wanted her to stay and die in *Menuchat Lev*. We wanted peace. We wanted her to be where she had grown familiar with things. We wanted it to be easy, just for a while, her end to be quick, and for everything not to get any worse. But we didn't believe that any of that would really happen.

We understood Mother would only get worse and that she would lose her abilities inch by inch, piece by piece. It became a slower process so when I visited her five or six times a year, I could track the changes better than Erika or Hannah. I think we all knew that she would go into the memory unit at some point, unless a fast illness took her sooner. But we were never quite sure when that time would be. It came when Mother began sundowning: dressing and trying to leave the assisted living facility at night. When she wandered the halls unaware of what time it was. It entailed another clearing out, another move that Erika and I handled.

I dreaded the moment she would no longer know me or Ivy. Would no longer happily say, "How *are* you, Leah?" when I rang her each week, even if she said, "how *are* you?" or "and so how are *you*?" over and over during each ten-minute phone call. She forgot her grandchildren first. Her children seemed to stay with her as people she knew but she wasn't quite sure of just who we were.

From the very beginning I felt like a traitor, a deceptor: When we finally got her into rehab, I never imagined that it would lead to her being banished from her home and her life forever. I had expected a good outcome, a better outcome. I hoped for a dried-out Mother, a well Mother able to go back home and live another ten or so years on her own, a Mother who had one last chance. Just any Mother other than the one we were left with. She had always been an accomplished actress. She could play the part of Good Mother with our friends, Glamorous Mother with our father, Loving Mother when one of us got sick. But there were layers and layers of other Mothers under her skin, like a closet packed with costumes one on top of another.

SHIVAH

For so long, we did not question who she was on a day-to-day basis. To try and dissect her subterfuge was simply too much. She had been such a force in our lives that it was easier, as the years went on and we were less and less tethered to her, to no longer wish to do the work of trying to understand what she was really saying, of trying to decipher the roles we played, she played, in her myriad moods. None of us wished to allow her that kind of power. We had our own lives to lead.

During those long and lonely years that preceded her actual diagnosis, Mother fooled her sister Hannah quite regularly. Hannah spoke with Mother nearly every day and saw her once a week, but I think she allowed herself to be fooled. She didn't want to think about the worst thing that could happen to her oldest sister. She didn't even want to consider the fact that Mother's drinking had become impossible. Hannah, who had known Mother as the cunning, difficult, demanding older sister who expected her sibling to bend to her every whim, broke down when the diagnosis was pronounced. She wept about it on and off for the rest of Mother's life. She continued to nurse a fantasy that Mother might rise once again from the ashes. Years after the diagnosis, after a particularly difficult holiday meal with Mother, Hannah sat, her hands playing with her glasses, and looked steadily into my eyes and said, "Your mother breaks my heart."

I resisted this. I wanted my heart never to be broken by her again.

Mother also fooled Erika every time she came to take

her out to lunch. Erika was like Hannah. Neither was adept at recognizing anything painful in the ones they loved. Their love was fierce and blind.

I was so wrapped up in my anger at Mother's drinking, so invested in maintaining my distance from her, that I could see nothing else. If, for some long time, years perhaps, Mother hadn't sounded or acted exactly normal, it was all relative. She sounded as normal as all of us expected her to. The blind mice. We were all the blind mice.

Nonetheless, it was a terrible thing for the three of us to watch as Mother began to really lose her *self*. It was like some sort of Mafia torture, but instead of fingers and toes being snipped off one by one, it was the larger bits of Mother's self: her brains, her wit, her ability to read, to concentrate, to track a conversation, her ability to make a decision. All the things she had prided herself on. She forgot how to use her computer, how to turn on her music, how to work the television. She didn't understand the telephone or who was on the other line. Instead of body parts being removed systematically, it was days. Days went, then weeks were gone; months disappeared, years completely evaporated. It was skills. It was ordinary movements, ordinary moments.

11.

During one visit to her, soon after the summer week with Paul, Mother, in a moment of incredible and terrible clarity, said to me, "You seem like you are in a good place in your life."

This kind of new age talk was not Mother. This kind of positive reinforcement was not Mother. The new Mother who occasionally presented herself to me after her diagnosis was certainly not the mother of my childhood imagination—she *might* have become somewhat kinder and more loving, somehow ask a probing question. But she was still just some weird manifestation of a disease that had robbed the mother I had gotten used to. Mother was the woman who called me promiscuous, selfish, and mean-spirited and who complained to her therapist that my sisters and I were out to destroy her. Mother was the woman who got angry when I, as a young, single woman, had refused to let her visit whenever she liked; Mother was the woman who threw temper tantrums on the street when she did come to visit.

Mother was selfish and solipsistic and only wanted to know about others' lives in relation to her own.

Mother was the woman who had spent the years of her children's childhood all but ignoring us, finding ways to put us out of her space. As very young babies, the three of us spent hours in playpens. Until we were school-aged we had been fed early and put to bed before dark so as not to disturb our father when he came home. It was really Mother who did not wish to be disturbed. Not by loud, demanding children, all close together in age but different as a bouquet of flowers.

By the beginning of the third year, I finally began to make peace with the fact that Old Mother was completely gone and that the new old lady with her ruined beauty and her lack of focus, the new old lady who told me she loved me over and over and over, who thanked me profusely for every visit, who sent large checks for holidays and birthdays and lavished all of us with the affection and attention none of us had experienced for the previous nearly fifty years, had replaced her. She was Mother. A sort of late-inning substitution.

Yet it was unnerving. The mean drunk, the alternately depressed and manic diva, the indifferent parent, the mother who had lived in a world of her own devising and dared others to doubt her interpretation had disappeared. Someone else had snatched her body.

Erika only said, "Yes, her new personality is strange," and Sara, took our parent changeling matter-of-factly. But

SHIVAH

for me, who had spent my whole childhood wishing I were an orphan who would eventually find my real parents and too much of my adulthood wishing for any kind of *other* mother, New Mother was almost as frightening as Old Mother. If I had the tools to deal with her new self, I had not yet enough history.

"My whole life I waited for her to tell me she loved me," I told Paul. "When she first started doing it, I thought it was just some cruel joke. Then I began to see that she means it, that she has to say it. Is it Mother or the alien inside her who is compelled to say such things?

"It feels too strange. I care and I don't. It's important and meaningless at the same time. She's turned into such a nice person. A nice person with whom one cannot carry on a conversation. It isn't horrible being with her anymore. But it is so damned sad."

"This is not the time to think about what she didn't say," Paul told me. "This is the time to be grateful for what she has *finally* said."

But that was easier said than done. The transformation was so astonishing that it transcended any explanation. With each larger piece of Mother that dropped off, a tiny feather of kindness, need, love and appreciation appeared. She was transforming, perhaps not in the way any of us would have wished, and it was as if her essential self, which had lain in waiting for seventy-five years, had finally been allowed to emerge. Had a good person been inside Mother all along? Was her anger and unhappiness just a cheap veneer that had finally chipped off? Was it hopeless or hopeful that I even considered that possibility? Or maybe was it really very simple: Mother's reality disintegrated and in its wake was something sweet but rotting, a flower held too long in a vase.

Years ago, I read some wisdom by Rabbi Schneur Zalman, a precursor of Freud by a hundred years. He counsels that dwelling on anger and childhood feelings of loss and abandonment is futile. He is quite clear that going deep into past feelings is useless. He cautions: "Don't be a fool to try to find the root of these thoughts and elevate them. This is only for the *tzaddikim*." The enlightened.

He has a point. I had been in therapy for years to try and rid myself of Mother's influence, but I was no closer to understanding her than I had ever been. It was evident I was no enlightened soul. I had neither the skills nor the grace to decipher Mother's motives or my attachment to them; the best I could do was break away and live my own life, which I had done—sometimes for better, sometimes for worse—for decades.

But Rabbi Zalman also poses a question that continues to haunt me: "But for the regular person, how can he raise his thoughts upward when he himself is tied below?" How do we, who are not the *tzaddikim*, find peace? His answer is not unlike the conclusion I came to with therapy: Raise yourself by your own efforts. I had tried. I had. And I think I mostly succeeded. The older I got the better I understood the value of just moving on. Even if it was possible to dissect the motives of others—and with Mother it simply was not—what good would it have ever done me? Having an answer would not have changed things.

Rabbi Zalman promises that with time, even the unenlightened of us might learn the tools to deal with anger, with sadness. He states that people only change when their problems become an obstacle to progress: "You cannot try and tame a dog while he is barking," he writes.

I experienced my obstacle to progress when I became a mother. As soon as I got pregnant with Ivy, I was struck by the obvious: I had neither the tools nor the history to be a mother. It was not in my DNA. If Alzheimer's was, motherhood was not. But it felt natural to be pregnant and to want a child, and the changes that began to come over me with the birth of Ivy were what finally helped me begin to let go of Mother and my past with her. Holding Ivy in my arms filled me with awe and responsibility—and with the deep knowledge that I had no useful tools. I could parent against how I had been raised, but was that enough?

Surely I had learned many positive things. I just had to untangle them from my own neuroses. I began to understand that even if I could never completely rid myself of the wounds of the past, the scars could fade such that they looked like the real scars from any surgery: Itching here and there just to let me know that I was neither invulnerable nor immortal but not so risen, so visible, so aching that I couldn't ignore them most of the time.

And then the dog stopped barking again all those years later. Who Mother became was my new lesson. I tried to be complacent, then pleased; Mother was finally expressing love and gratitude. It was hard, but I accepted the statements as true.

I told her I loved her, too. And the more I said it the truer it became.

The Condolence Meal

If possible, the first meal after burial is prepared by friends to be eaten alone by the grieving family.

"There are times when parenthood seems nothing more than feeding the hand that bites you."
—Peter De Vries

1.

For most of her married life, Mother kept back money from the household account—the money my father gave her for groceries, children's lessons and needs, clothes and the like—so that when she finally left the marriage, she had several thousand dollars in the bank. It wasn't nearly enough for anything, really, and certainly did not help her in the mental institution where she transitioned from married life to single life, but it was enough to make Mother feel better. Her miserliness had always been a source of comfort for her.

She and Father separated but they did not immediately divorce and during this period, Father sent Mother money every month. When they finally did divorce, he made her a generous settlement, but Mother would spend the rest of her conscious time worrying about how much money she had and how much money she could spend. It was ironic, then perhaps fitting, that the remains of those accounts enabled her to live independently until her death.

What if she had been profligate and spent all her money while she still had her mind? That was something I didn't even want to think about. Father, who had also grown up during the Depression and in even poorer circumstances than Mother, had trouble spending money on himself, but never any trouble spending it on others. He was always quick to pick up a check. Mother spent most of her life heading to the ladies' room as soon as the meal was over and reappearing mysteriously after the bill was paid. She was tight with gifts, tight with affection, tight with anything that could possibly be given away. During the last years before her diagnosis, she told me more than once that her biggest fear was becoming a bag lady. She defended this obsession by telling me that Gloria Steinem also had the same fear.

"I think hers is symbolic, Mother," I said. "I think she is trying to say that most women are so very close to penury that they don't even realize it. If their husband dies or something happens to pull the rug out from under them, they could indeed be on the street. But that's unlikely to happen to you. Besides," I added, perhaps a little meanly at the time, "Steinem never had any children to take care of her in her old age."

Mother had her odd quirks, though. Things she would spend money on, no matter what. Never one to have extra tchotchkes—no pairs of shoes she hardly ever wore, no extra handbag—for much of her life she did have an obsession with food, especially with running out of it. It wasn't that she particularly liked to eat it. Nor did she like cooking. But she needed to have food around her. We should have realized when her house became so empty of groceries it was a signal that something had gone very haywire.

In one of our late-night talks during a visit to see Mother, Hannah told me that Mother's obsession stemmed from the fact that her parents had run out of food at her wedding. Among even lower middle-class American Jews, that was completely unthinkable. It was the ultimate *shanda*, the largest shame. Mother never forgot her mortification; the shame of that memory would haunt her forever. Mother always made far too much to feed even a family of five: Her leftovers had leftovers. At least one night each week everything that had been partially eaten some night earlier was heated up and brought to the table as dinner. Even the tiniest bits had been saved.

Although she had been raised as an Orthodox Jew, Mother was moved by her husband and marriage to a small town in Tennessee, a state she hadn't even known existed. Once there, she found keeping kosher impossible. After a couple of years, she gave up even the appearance of it: The groceries shipped down on trains from up north came spoiled. The local supermarkets in the South in the fifties and sixties were full of nothing but canned, frozen and packaged foods—and *trafe*, plenty of *trafe*. And even though Mother liked to consider herself a serious cook, she hated the role and performed it gracelessly.

And the dinner table, even with its studied largess,

was always a battleground, not a sanctuary. Father wanted nothing more than to eat his meals in peace and quiet while Mother demanded meaningful, intelligent conversation from all involved. She requested interesting tidbits from her husband's day at work. Father fought back, insisting his days on the road or in the office offered nothing funny or of interest to tell. Mother was convinced otherwise: Surely what he was doing all day must be more challenging, more fascinating, more important and meaningful than the way her days were spent. He had been out all day in the world. His silence infuriated her.

Fed separately and put to bed early well into grade school, when my sisters and I were finally invited to the adult table, the expectations Mother placed on us were simply too much. For a long time we picked at each other and started silly fights, just as we had when we sat alone. As we got older, we were collectively sullen and not forthcoming, even when asked questions, although Erika, the youngest, would occasionally try valiantly to entertain. Later, as teenagers, Sara and I would come to the table stoned and pride ourselves on getting away with it, on the obliviousness of our parents. We didn't realize that they were so wrapped up in themselves we could have been tripping on acid and they wouldn't have noticed.

Anything our parents said was foolish or uninteresting, anyway. And there was always the added possibility that any night could be one of the nights when Mother, for reasons no one could fathom, would suddenly burst into tears or leave the table in a fury. There were also the many nights Mother stood in the kitchen, nibbling from a pot of spaghetti sauce or soup, not quite making it to the table. My father sat with us. She alternated between demanding conversation and engagement and removing herself from the picture completely.

At an early age, I was aware that our dinner table was not normal. I suspected that a lot of families, even then, watched television or ate hurried meals so as to go off and do other more interesting things. Eating together was not the kind of sacred act the rabbis envisioned when they turned the home into a tabernacle substitute. It was bad theatre, a battle, a punishment characterized by Mother's goading to speak up and be interesting and steady, angry silence. I still have a photograph of me crying at the table because I did not want supper. This was in the days when one had to go and get a camera, take the photo and then have it printed. It was only when I became a mother that I began to appreciate my own mother's efforts to cook fresh, good food and encourage conversation, even if the way she went about it made us all feel like we were on stage. Feeding my own family, I began to appreciate the way my mother had tried. I avoided her less admirable habits: the goading, the expectation of scintillating conversation, the tantrums. But it seemed a good, if slightly outmoded idea, to sit at the table and share a well-cooked meal.

After Mother's diagnosis, reading a menu became one of

the first things her mind jettisoned; it presented too many possibilities and the agony of too many decisions. But we wanted to take her out of *Menuchat Lev* for our visits. I needed to—on my visits I needed to get out of the place as much as possible—so I just ordered for her, brightly, cheerfully, encouragingly. She behaved like Ivy had as a child; Mother played with her egg salad sandwiches, she crushed the potato chips into bits, even as we cajoled her, to please take one more bite. Begged her to please just eat a little bit.

Her trim figure had always been a source of pride, but it wasn't until we grew much older and put the pieces together that I realized Mother's weight consumed her. I recalled the pink plastic enema bag that hung always on the bathroom door and the packages of laxatives in all the medicine cabinets—those same laxatives that showed up on Mother's endless shopping lists the first couple of years she was living at *Menuchat Lev*. Her constant purging ruined her bowels, which presented an issue the sicker she got. But her inability to enjoy food, her need to control it, meant that she was the one person who had immediately recognized Pam's anorexia, long before the term *eating disorder* entered popular usage.

Yet, despite the incessant skirmishes at the dinner table, or perhaps because of them, my sisters and I all grew to be fine cooks who liked food and enjoyed preparing it. Sara may have been the only one of us who did it professionally—and I always envied the way she could bone a chicken in an instant, could hunt and kill a deer and then bleed it and dress it, the way she could cook rabbit, moose, bear—but the three of us shared menus and traded recipes, bragging about a particular accomplishment. And each of us, when we were first on our own, took a kind of bizarre pride in feeding Mother when she visited, concocting recipes more complicated each time. It was passive-aggressive behavior at its pinnacle, but it didn't really matter what we made because Mother ate so little. The first time she went to Sanderstone after her breakdown, she lost at least twenty pounds, which on her frame was a lot; she had always been quite slim. She never gained the weight back.

2.

When Mother had her breakdown, her best friend called Hannah and told her she couldn't get Mother out of bed; it had been a week and Mother was catatonic. Hannah dropped everything, flew down and brought Mother back up to Sanderstone. She saved her life.

Four years earlier when I started college nearby, Hannah saved mine when she adopted me into the large and welcoming extended family she and her husband Sam shared. She took me in and welcomed me with no-strings-attached love; with her warm graciousness and her willingness to both listen and confide, she had been the mother I would have chosen had I been given the chance. Through the four years I was in college and the several years after when I lived in Boston, I was always invited to Hannah's for Thanksgiving and every major Jewish holiday. Hannah was the force who dispelled the notion that the dining table had to be a battlefield. She was the one who first showed me a way to offer food with real love—I could not have become the cook I am without her as model. For all the years I was in New England, her home was mine. All the years I made trips up alone and then with my own small family to see Mother, I visited Hannah, and her house was a welcome respite.

Hannah was right there when Mother checked into Sanderstone for the second time, and her spare beds were made up whenever I came up to see Mother at *Menuchat Lev*, whether I traveled alone, with Ivy, or with Ivy and Paul. Her fridge was stocked with whatever things she remembered I had said I liked. Her house always looked the same, smelled the same, hugged me as I walked in the front door.

Like the most perfect of mothers, like the kind of mother one could only fashion in a fairy tale or fiction, she gave everything and asked nothing. We would sit for hours around her kitchen table, talking about anything that moved us. I knew I idealized Hannah, that she was as flawed as the rest of us, but she had been so polar opposite to Mother, had remained so relentlessly upbeat despite her own tsuris—issues with her children, issues with her health, her father's early death, her mother's illness, her husband Sam's illness, Mother's diagnosis and needs—that I needed to be near her. I needed to absorb some of her placid kindness, some of her unflappability, even if it was partially a figment of my own imagination, born out of my own desire for stability.

I knew Hannah wished more out of her own life. More than once, over late-night drinks at her kitchen table, she confessed lost opportunities, missed moments, lamented the fact that circumstances had prevented her moving very far from where she had grown up. But Hannah accepted her own decline with graciousness and humor. Her happiness had never been contingent on just one other person: She gathered love around her in bunches. Her soul was intact and that was something to which I aspired.

When Mother moved back north after her breakdown, she became a guest at Hannah's for every holiday meal. And Hannah had a lot of holidays: Thanksgiving, Passover, the breaking of the fast at Yom Kippur, Mother's Day, Father's Day, birthdays, and anything else Hannah felt like celebrating. Too often, Mother repaid Hannah's kindness by drinking too much. But Hannah had always been the glue that held her own family together—her children, grandchildren, and then great-grandchildren, aunts and uncles, nieces and nephews, cousins—and she was damned if she wouldn't continue to welcome anyone who needed her into the mix, even her own sick sister.

Mother went from being jealous and abusive when drinking too much to wandering the rooms and stealing wine from others' glasses after she became sick. She would ask to immediately be taken home. Yet Hannah would continue to send Sam to pick Mother up for any special occasion and sometimes even on a whim, even though she knew well how difficult it might be. As time progressed, while the invitations did not stop, whenever possible, Erika or I were invited to come and sit with Mother to monitor her wine consumption and her behavior. I marveled at Hannah's good-hearted willingness to put up with Mother's *mishegas*: Having Mother to the house was like actually inviting *in* the elephant.

For the first few years, Mother seemed happy enough, if often disoriented, to go to Hannah's. Three years into her disease Mother began to find more and more excuses not to go: She was ill or tired or it was too late.

"I don't think she feels comfortable out of her environment anymore," Hannah told me. Erika had noticed the same thing happening more and more when she took Mother out to lunch. The music would be too loud; the air conditioning too cool; the heat too high; the place too noisy with frivolity; Mother could find nothing on the menu to suit her. But if Hannah did not invite Mother, Mother would complain she never saw her. If Erika neglected to take her out, Mother would complain that she never went anywhere.

At *Menuchat Lev*, an old childhood friend, who by great coincidence lived in the apartment across from her, left Mother a muffin each morning outside her door so that she would have something in her stomach when she slept through breakfast, which she often did. He and other residents stopped by her rooms to make sure she made her way to the dining room for meals. They watched her like hawks to make sure that she ate something, no matter how little.

"Your mother doesn't eat," they would say, shaking their heads at me whenever I would come to *Menuchat Lev* for a meal. Mother would roll her eyes and then when she was alone with me would complain: "The food is terrible!" But the fact that the food was, at best, mediocre was not why Mother did not eat it. Like so much else that was lost to her, it simply had no meaning to her, even when others prepared it. She did not understand the intention or desire of others to nurture her. The women who served her at *Menuchat Lev* would shake their heads as they took her plate. "Honey," they would say, "is that *all* you're gonna eat?"

As though she would even be able to give them an intelligible answer.

3.

By the end of the first year at *Menuchat Lev*, Mother reigned as queen bee, as if she were royalty in exile: the real Anastasia. Her silence or indifference or both became more profound, but as old and ill as she was, the vestiges of her former regal beauty were still visible. Her personality, even diminished, was still somehow formidable. Her ego, still seemingly intact behind the shuttered and locked windows of her mind, could still propel people to both anticipate and carry out her demands. She could command attention even if she did it unawares. When she could still speak, she knew all the residents by name or sight and was scarcely ever in her room when I called her. (I could not leave a message as she had forgotten how to access her answering machine. She had already lost the use of her computer and her radio and CD player. The television she could manage as long as it stayed on the channel it was playing when she turned it on.)

Those first few years, Mother wandered the halls for hours saying hello to everyone, stopping in the lobby and sitting by the fireplace to read the same *Providence Journal*, the same *Boston Globe*, over and over. In warmer weather, she walked the grounds and deadheaded the cosmos, marigolds, petunias as if they were her own, dropping the expired flowers like Hansel and Gretel's breadcrumbs. That first year I could never be sure if she knew where she was and was denying it or if she had accepted the new place as her real home. She simply didn't talk about much of anything. Six months after we sold her house, she never mentioned it again.

I watched in amazement the way the other residents catered to my shell of a mother. There was something so awful and tragic about it. But something enviable and beautiful. She was the center of attention, which she would have adored, had always adored. But she had no way to process it.

I understood why, at the end fairy tales, princesses ride off into the sunset never to be heard from again. That way they preserve their beauty: They are still young and lovely, still alive. Viewing the decline of anyone, even a woman part witch and part princess, was painful.

Before her final illness, when Mother was in one of her manic phases in her first illness, she had been so huge, so present, so very alive. Even her depressive cycles were incredibly dramatic, scripted like something out of Williams or Albee—entertaining, I supposed, but only if you were part of the audience and not on stage with her. But this part she was playing now, to her end, to *the* end, was to a captive audience that had never seen her before and that had no idea of who she had been.

It took several years for the last remnants of the furious woman she had been to dissipate completely, but those moments happened mostly in private. The brunt of her anger seemed to be directed at Hannah and her husband, Sam. At the beginning, Sam drove Hannah over often and he himself checked in on her weekly. In the first two years, when Mother complained about having to ride the residence bus to the symphony, he picked her up. But she took their kindness as though it was a given. In her narcissism she had always expected people to do for her.

During the twenty-five years she was in her own home, Mother presumed upon Sam by asking him to do things she could have hired out. He was needed to do simple tasks she could have learned herself. When she was denied, everyone around her was made miserable. And Sam and Hannah, with their myriad connections, were the ones who got a place for Mother so quickly at *Menuchat Lev*. While she thanked my sisters and me, she never expressed that to Hannah or Sam. She only accused them of trying to get rid of her. For Hannah, it grew less and less desirable to see Mother, as much as she mourned the absence. It was too draining. Sometimes she would wait until I came up to visit so that she could go with me and make the visit easier; it was always easier when there was another person around to help pass the excruciating time with Mother.

Even though Mother complained of her new kingdom, complained that Sam and Hannah tried to get rid of her, *Menuchat Lev* was not a place of exile. It was a brand-new, freshly built, state-of-the-art facility, the best of its kind around. There were Friday night lay-led services, a roster of activities including music, films and lectures. There were day trips to Newport and the beaches. A bus ran to the theatre and the symphony and took residents out shopping two days a week. The lobby looked like an old English seaside hotel with overstuffed chairs and a gas fireplace. There was an exercise room, a hairdresser, medical staff, a beautiful dining room and a coffee shop. If I didn't look too closely at the men in wheelchairs, the women with their walkers, if I had not heard the story of one of Mother's dinner companions dropping dead as he rose from the table, I could almost . . . It wasn't such a *bad* place. If Mother had to be in such a place, it was the place to be. And what were the other options when she had refused to leave New England? Send her out on an ice floe?

4.

One evening, well into Mother's third year at *Menuchat Lev*, I was talking to Paul about how I still felt guilty for not realizing Mother had Alzheimer's earlier. It continued to trouble me that I didn't go up and see her often enough. I told him I thought I had failed her somehow.

He turned to me and said, as angry as I had ever seen him, "You have not failed *her*. She failed *you*. All of you. Please remember that."

I tried to explain to him that the farther and farther I got from the mother I had known, the harder it got to remember how she had failed me. I grieved the loss of her such a long time ago, before she had ever gotten Alzheimer's. I had effectively already sat Shivah. Or so I thought. I was finally at peace with the fact that she had been sick all of my life and that her actions were part of her illness, not just capricious and careless behaviors designed to wound as deeply as possible. It was all part of the complex web of mental instability that Mother tried as hard as she could to put to rest by drinking. I didn't blame her any longer, but I had stopped expecting anything from her other than the most rudimentary decency, even if that most rudimentary of decent behavior was often beyond her.

When sitting Shivah, we are admonished by the rabbis not to be carried away by grief. We must not let our grief consume us: It does a grave disservice to the immortality of the dead soul. And the time for sitting Shivah is carefully circumscribed: There is a week full of mourning, a month when certain rituals must be applied, and a year before the headstone is placed on the grave. After all that, we are admonished to get on with our lives as a testament to the living, rather than continue our mourning. But Shivah wasn't meant for her disease, and as I watched Mother break apart piece by piece by piece, I grieved each sliver that fell to the ground. It was like mourning broken shards of glass.

How does one mourn vestiges of a person? Whatever was left of Mother dissipated as quickly as the morning fog on the mountain: impenetrable and then gone.

When the view cleared, I saw that there was increasingly little of Mother left.

5.

"Erika's upset that Mother won't stop drinking," I told Paul after I got off the phone with her. Mother had been at *Menuchat Lev* for nearly six years and was still managing, somehow, to cadge a ride to a store up the street that sold wine. She even ordered it with an old credit card we had forgotten to take away. Her cunning was amazing, considering she barely spoke.

"She's always upset."

"You're right about that, but Erika wants me to say something to Mother."

"Like what?"

"I have no idea. I can't think why she thinks anything I would say would make a difference."

"Good God, Leah," Paul sighed. "There is nothing to say. Is there? I mean, wouldn't you drink, too? If you were in her situation?"

"Well, probably," I said. "I don't know. I don't know what it's like to either be a drunk or to lose my mind. I would like to think that by this point I would be already dead. That you would have smothered me with a pillow."

Paul laughed.

"I am perfectly serious," I said. "I expect you to help me do myself in." Paul ignored me. I knew he hated talk like that. He hated for me to even talk about how much it scared me to think about getting Alzheimer's. I turned back to the subject at hand.

"Okay," I said. "But don't you think she would be better if she would stop drinking? Maybe then the medicine would have more effect? The disease's progress might slow. That's what I've read. The Aricept won't work with the alcohol. I don't know why they give that drug to her anyway. I don't think the doctors have any idea how much she drinks."

"I think you need to leave her alone," Paul said. "If she wants to drink, let her drink. How the hell are you going to stop her anyway?"

I looked hard at Paul. "Mother told me when she was first diagnosed and started back in drinking that wine was the only pleasure she had left."

"If that's true," Paul said, "she had damned well *better* drink."

I couldn't bring myself to tell Erika what Mother had said. It would make Erika even more angry. Erika continued to worry and ask me what I thought. I continued to avoid her question and not think about what I thought. Erika was sure that Mother would be kicked out of *Menuchat Lev*. And then what would we do? And sure enough, one day Erika called me, in a frenzy.

"She fell down the other day," Erika said. "They called and told me. She was drunk, drunk at dinner. Shit-faced drunk."

"I don't know what to tell you," I said wearily. "She's been drinking for forty years."

"But she stopped!"

"Yes, and then look what happened."

Of course they didn't kick her out. She stayed upstairs until she began to sundown: to dress in her clothes and wander the halls at night, trying to leave by the front door. Then we moved her into the memory unit with its locked doors and patients who made you ache deep in your bones when you saw them.

The Telling of Stories

A Shivah house can be quiet but it can also be a welcome place for mourners to share photographs and narratives of the deceased.

"Without memory, souls become brittle and vulnerable."
—from a Passover Haggadah

1.

Before Mother's diagnosis, I often told people stories of what had happened to my sisters and me when we were children, but with each passing year, I was so far away from them that the stories began to feel like they belonged to someone else entirely. Also, I felt bad about telling stories about my mother when she was incapacitated by no memory. It seemed weirdly cruel. And over time it became apparent, that too often, my sisters and I disagreed on what really happened, on the seriousness of an event or the details or who was ultimately responsible.

So I am done with the stories. This is the final telling.

The thing about Alzheimer's is that there is no plot to it: No beginning, middle or end. There is no denouement, no rising action, climax or falling action. The resolution doesn't come at the end. All the points converge from the moment the disease is diagnosed. It is rather the way Alain Robbe-Grillet told his readers to approach his novels: Start anywhere, he said, read front to back, or back to front; start in the middle and read outward either way. It's all the same. The book will make as much sense in any order one chooses. Mother always demurred that what she didn't know could not hurt her. As a result, my sisters and I spent most of our youth lying by omission. No outright fibs were told, but we left out a lot. We left out all the good stuff.

Perhaps that history of saying almost nothing made me yearn for revelation. Since her diagnosis and her death, I have searched for the truth and the courage to say it. But convinced of truth's inherent goodness I realized that I had often been too careless with it. In thinking it was always a good weapon to wield, I never quite understood, never wished to even think about the fact, that there are many people for whom pointing out that the emperor is naked is more cruel than pretending he looks wondrous in his finery.

2.

As the story goes, in the mid-1950s, my father married my mother and brought her down to the small mill town in Appalachia in which we grew up (*ek velt*, she called it, the boondocks). I think she might have been better if she'd had her breakdown right there and then—at the beginning. She did not. She had three children in a row and then she set about being what she had never really wanted to be: A housewife who dabbled. She was not very good at either the housewifery or the dabbling: Both were beneath her.

My parents were a handsome, glamorous, intelligent, and fairly sophisticated couple. They radiated a kind of untouchable energy: Heat, light, and flash. They had met briefly in college and then gone off, separately, to New York City: Mother to work as a low-level assistant at Simon and Schuster, Father as a copy boy for the *New York Daily News*. Then he split for Paris to be a writer.

Discouraged by his poverty and lack of talent, he headed back to the States to work for his uncles in rural East

Tennessee. He needed a wife. He remembered my mother whom he had met a few times in the coffee room at the university library, where they both drank their coffee black and smoked cigarettes between studying. He thought my mother glamorous and smart and well bred. He proposed, and she accepted. He was twenty-eight and she was twenty-five. As it was at the time, he was a handsome bachelor, she was well on her way to becoming an old maid.

And so there they found themselves, plunked down in a poor, small town in the middle of nowhere where they became part of the mid-1950's Southern diaspora of Jews displaced from New York, Massachusetts, Connecticut and other points north, all of whom were somehow connected to the booming furniture trade. Maybe, if Mother had just had the courage to wait out marriage for a dozen more years or so, she might have been able to be on her own. It might have been a more acceptable thing to be a career woman. But I don't think she would have made it without a husband because there was a streak of conventionality in her; she needed to do the done thing. Like having several children. But at times in my life, her strength surprised me. She managed to put her life back together after a breakdown; she managed to sit, without conscious mortification, with a horrific disease. And so, Mother might well have been better off without the shoulder of a man to lean on. Like most women, leaning on someone else did not become her.

It wasn't that Mother had not wanted to get married, although she hadn't really, or that she was opposed to moving so far away from her job in New York City—which she saw as the center of the universe—although she was, actually, or even that she was frightened and lonely, which she most certainly was. It wasn't, in all evidence, that she didn't love my father: She did, at first, quite a lot. But even though he was the man she had wished for, even though her dreams of going to a good college, meeting a handsome Jewish man, gaining economic stability and status all came true, her dreams hadn't been honest ones. I think those are the things she thought she should wish for. The things she secretly wished for (to be a famous actress or writer, to be acclaimed for some enormous talent, or, more crucially, to be in another person's skin entirely—a person who did not feel her pain) were completely untenable. She had been neither brave enough nor sane enough to choose the road less taken, and I grew to finally understand it was not her fault.

As the story goes, my father spent most of his time making money, which he was very good at. Under a nom de plume, Mother wrote a blithe and breezy weekly newspaper column for the local paper. She volunteered, she joined clubs, she did some acting in the local theater. Mostly, though, she was *oysgematert*. Exhausted. *Oysgematert* all the time.

It was very early in her marriage when Mother took up drink to elevate the joy and alleviate the pain. At first, it was a five o'clock scotch with my father. Later, vodka disguised in orange juice or iced tea. Still later, cheap white wine. She drank black coffee from the moment she woke until lunch time and then she began drinking. Father joined her in her cocktails when he returned home from work, and throughout our youth, the two of them danced and drank and made noisy love behind locked doors, had elaborate parties with dress-up outfits, fancy cocktails and complicated hors d'oeuvres.

As Father grew more successful, they traveled, leaving the three of us with a series of unsuitable older women who were nearly as indifferent as our parents: I watched *Imitation of Life* with one of the babysitters. I was ten. It was completely inappropriate but soon became one of my favorite movies. But none of that revelry or distraction was enough to appease Mother. And none of the joy was enough to make up for my father's diminishing expectations. Mother was too much work for him; he was too little of everything for her.

It was possible that for many years Mother may not have even realized how ill she was, even as she suffered huge moments of mania punctuated by long days and weeks of terrible sadness. No doctors were called, no pills other than tranquilizers were taken. I never knew why. I asked my father once why he left his children in the care of a crazy woman and he just shrugged: She was the mother, he went to work, that was the way it was. That Mother did not take care of her children, his children, never even registered with him.

Not only did he not dissuade Mother from her behavior, he was not even a buffer. He placated her when she was down, until it bored him. When she was up, he rode beside her, enjoying the energy. But he was not the kind of man to ride in, like Prince Charming on his white horse, and rescue us. We were just the detritus of his marriage. And Mother? She was part dragon and part smoke.

3.

When we cleaned out her house and I found an old red leatherette journal that Mother kept in high school and through her first years in college, the sparse entries were illuminating. Mother was born unhappy, born with a birth defect: A terminal melancholia, physical and emotional.

In the early entries Mother's sadness was palpable; it leapt off the page. She felt lonely, unloved, ugly. Many of the days were marked by a longing for love and normalcy, by a crying out for beauty and friendship, by pages and pages of woe is me. I knew I had felt the same way, too, at times. What teenage girl hadn't? But that sadness never left her, save for the moments when she danced like a madwoman. For all her beauty and intelligence, for all the sacrifices her parents had made to send her to college, for the good fortune to have healthy children, a loving husband, money, the means to travel and see the world, none of that was enough to dissipate her unhappiness: The sadness won out over everything.

The tone in that journal from so long ago was the same

as that which marked the letters she sent me, the same as her later journals, the ones that chronicled Mother's adult life—her life up until the day she got the diagnosis. The pages were all anger: A feeling that life had happened *to* her, in spite of herself. Her children were out to get her, her husband had conspired to leave her penniless, no one would cut her a break.

When I was a senior in college, my mother's life suddenly took a turn for the worse, according to her telling years later. Her story is that up until then everything had been pretty much fine. She hadn't even realized what was happening. She said she just couldn't get her life back on course. Hence the breakdown. Hence her separation, which, ten years later, became a divorce. But her stories were hard to believe because later, all evidence to the contrary, she publicly insisted she had been perfectly happy all those years with my father in Tennessee. Years and years after the divorce but well before the diagnosis, she even tried to tell me that she had never wanted to leave Tennessee at all.

Perhaps her desire to divorce had been just a threat. She never really expected Father to agree. He called her bluff. But even separated, they still saw each other and traveled together occasionally for years until they finally divorced.

4.

Even after the divorce was finalized, my parents kept in touch. They still cared about each other, especially when both of them were dying at the same time. Hundreds of miles away from Mother in assisted living, my father continued to die by tortuous inches. His was a total system failure: He had a weak heart, no lungs; he had survived, barely, five strokes and at least three heart attacks. He was being kept alive by sheer force of will, his new wife's, and his own reluctance to believe that his body was so betraying him. He was on full-time oxygen and would be for the rest of his life. He had a walker. Most of the time, he batted away help and then barked orders like an infirm Napoleon.

Those were several blurry years when I felt that all I did was travel between my parents and their illnesses, not having any idea what to expect at any time. The moment of death was always at hand. My sisters and I would get calls that my father wasn't doing well or had been taken to the hospital (broken rib, collapse, fever, anything and everything) and we would rush to see him, wandering the puke green halls of the hospital trying to find his room number. This went on for years, while to see Mother, I planned regular visits, carefully spaced, every three months. Each time, I knew it could be my last.

I didn't resent either of my parent's illnesses, their slow and agonizing dyings. There was not much they could do about any of it, buffeted as they were by the winds of chance and the ministrations of those who were responsible for them. No one wanted to be the one whose hand was directly pushing the end button. But the coincidence seemed profound. Father had most of his mind but his body was failing him daily; Mother's body was strong but her mind was lost. Together the two of them made a whole person. It had always been thus: the two of them making up for each other's deficiencies as parents but not quite succeeding in the long run.

Father always asked about Mother and she always asked about him. For a while I told the truth to each of them but it caused too much distress. I had to stop telling Mother about each new medical crisis in Father's life because it made her sad. "Your poor father," she would say over and over. "Your poor, poor father."

My father seemed equally overcome. When I visited him soon after Mother went to live at *Menuchat Lev*, he asked me how she was.

"She has Alzheimer's," I said.

"Well," he paused. "So, how is she?" Then he began to

cry.

Two years after my father died, I was up visiting Mother. We were eating dinner in a restaurant and Mother, in unusually good humor, smiled broadly and said, "I wish your father could have lived long enough to see what a beautiful and intelligent woman you turned out to be." I was fifty-four at the time of his death.

5.

In my youth I had no knowledge of her underlying illness and no consciousness yet of how much she drank to try and make her life palatable. I didn't know what children know now through the osmosis of just living. From television and movies. Oh how the media can make them wise. I was constantly looking for explanations. I wove scenarios. I needed desperately to understand that her behavior was not purely arbitrary, but what I came up with was so little. I knew so little.

    I have adapted to this new information age so well that sometimes I need to remind myself my youth took place before the ubiquity of cable television, the internet, and twenty-four-hour news. The only information I had about families came from the very little television we were allowed to watch: The black and white dramas starring perfect mothers like June Cleaver, Donna Reed and Margaret Anderson. If they seemed more desirable than the mother to whom I had been born, I was smart enough to also realize they were pretty boring: The dramas played out in those living rooms were nothing like the ones played out in ours. Not getting a date for the prom seemed like a small price to pay for the girls in those families who had everything else. And, of course, everything worked out in the end. The desirable boy called, the cad was called out: Happy endings all around. On television, the parents did know best.

As a child, I read a lot, but normal families were not what I read about. I liked historical novels about dead people. But if I knew that something wasn't quite right, I didn't really know how wrong it was. I wasn't at all sure what the norm for family was and dysfunction did not litter the airwaves as it does now. There were no touchstones by which to measure ourselves.

6.

My parents worried their marriage like an old scab, picking at it, exposing it, letting it heal, opening it up again. My father said Mother nagged; Mother said my father ignored her except in bed. My father said Mother never forgave him for not being an artist; Mother said her husband left all the child-rearing to her while he went off and had a life. All of this was true. Mother had married a man she thought was creative and had, instead, gotten a businessman, albeit a businessman who provided for her every need and a lot of her whims. Her children, as much as she wished them not to, consumed her in ways she would never have thought possible.

But even people who knew some little part about Mother's issues still thought she and my father were the perfect couple. Until my parents so publicly imploded. It might have seemed sudden to onlookers, but to my sisters and me, who had been waiting for years for the bomb to go off, my father getting an apartment up the road wasn't much of a surprise. When I was fifteen, I overheard Mother confess to her best friend—the same best friend that took up with Father during his separation from Mother—that she had married to have sex. Mother wanted to have sex but she said she just couldn't bring herself to do it outside of marriage. When Father offered marriage, she jumped in with both feet. It was another good story for me to remember and tell. I have no idea how much, if any of it, was true.

The first time I came home from college to visit, Father ran into my old bedroom and swept all of his stuff off the bureau. He seemed embarrassed and told me he had been sleeping in my room because his snoring bothered Mother. A few months after the actual separation, Mother had the nervous breakdown she had been putting off for years, and she was rescued by Hannah and checked into Sanderstone. Her recovery was slow but nearly miraculous. She came out of it just as angry and put upon, just as furious at the world as before she had broken down. I never realized how much she was still waiting, waiting for some*thing*, some*one* to happen to her.

Tucked into a pile of old letters from my mother to my father I found one that ended like this:

> *I love you, love you, you hear? I love you.*
> *I adore you. I miss you like fury. I love you.*

SHIVAH

But in a later journal I found this:

It happened again today. My husband and I were having lunch at the local country club and talking, talking through lunch, after lunch, well after most of the other guests had left. Three times, different people approached our table and commented, in more or less the same words: "Well, lovebirds, it's good to see married people so interested in each other."

We have been talking this way for weeks, at home, in restaurants, at the club where I sometimes meet him when I can take time from my work and he from his. What the spectators, the envious commentators don't know is that we are talking about the condition of our marriage and whether or not there is anything worth salvaging. After twenty years we are talking, analyzing, dissecting, bringing up great dead weights that have lain gathering the mold of irritation, dissatisfaction, anger, and scraping them off to see what is underneath. Better we should have done it years ago before the weights accumulated, but we do it now. We find it easier to talk in public. I don't cry and he doesn't clam up or raise his voice. We just talk. The coffee grows cold, the cigarettes pile up in the ashtrays which the waitress empties again and again.

And married couples point at us, whisper about us. "See, married such a long time and they still find things to say to each other."

Still? Some of the things are being said for the first time, some for the thousandth. Are we better off the way we are or better if we separate? Do we hurt each other more together than if we were apart? Is his desire for peace and warmth equal to mine for excitement and stimulus? Is his need for detachment greater than mine for commitment?

"Oh, it's nice to see people still interested in being together."
Yes. It is. Isn't it?

Mother took a lover sometime toward the end of her marriage, a lover who completely consumed her, who was the

SHIVAH

kind of man she thought she deserved: A handsome, erudite professor. But that way lay madness, too. She threw all her eggs in his basket, and he left her. I found some carbons she made of letters to him. They were incoherent, crazy. If anything, her love for him drove her closer toward complete madness. No man she ever met after even began to fill his shoes.

7.

My mother was unsettled in her time: the women's movement made her angry. Feminism appeared when she wasn't quite yet ready—she was raising young children in a backward Southern town. But at the same time feminism came too late for a woman who had already made the choices that locked her into a life she wasn't sure of.

She would rail constantly against the options my sisters and I had. That was the word Mother used, *options*: The word as curse. "I am so glad we did not have the options that you girls today have," she would say. "How on earth can you choose among so many choices?" She acted like our choices were as numerous as the kinds of breakfast cereals or shampoos on supermarket shelves. We weren't even sure what our options were. Mostly we felt our options consisted of just getting out of town and going to college; we had yet to discover how really different our lives could be if we let them. Or how very many chapters we would live in our lives. How things could ebb and flow, change direction, how we could move from place to place, love to love. But rather than educate us, be glad for us, and guide us, Mother was just envious and venomous. She was furious at our ability to speak our minds; she didn't wish to listen to any of our complaints because hers were more important. She seemed nervous that someone might actually listen to us, take us seriously when she felt no one had done that with her.

She saw our rebellion, if that was what it even was, our desire to not automatically give over our lives to one man and a marriage, as a personal affront to her. She didn't make marriage or monogamy look good or fun or desirable, but she wished it on us anyway. We had heard the stories of her own former boyfriends: A Communist her parents forbade her to see, a handsome actor who became a minor television star. She would drop this information carelessly into conversation when she wore a piece of jewelry the communist had given her or when the famous actor appeared on television. She wanted us to be sure she once had been something more than our mother, but she also wanted us to know what she had given up. When I reached middle age, my best beauty lost, and saw my gorgeous young daughter ready to take my place in the eyes of men, I understood her insecurity, her anxiety, her pathos. But she was so desperate about it all.

I think Mother would have liked to be Susan Sontag or someone like her; Mother would have liked to stay in the city, to take lovers. She would have liked to work in some fringy glamorous job. Had she been able. I have no idea if her fragile mental health would have permitted that sort of life:

She might have gone famously off her rocker, or she might well have stabilized if she lived the life she had imagined.

Deep down, I believe that if she stayed in New York, she still would have drowned. She would have drowned, but she might not have taken so many people down with her. As it was, her husband, her children, her sisters, her friends, we all tiptoed around Mother for years, trying not to "get her started" in one fit of pique or another, on a crying jag, or a locked bedroom session.

8.

Despite all evidence to the contrary, Mother would sigh deeply and say that she wanted more children but that her husband wouldn't hear of it. Father always countered that it seemed to him that three of us were three more than she could handle. We children were, as is always the case with children, a Janus gift, but Mother took to motherhood peculiarly badly. She parented alternately by despair and joy; if she was happy, her children were perfect; if she was sad, we were sent from hell to destroy her. There was no consistency and never an apology.

Mother gave us nothing but mixed signals: One day we were the best little girls in the world, the next we could do nothing right. She smothered us in a blanket of something like love that Mother was convinced was comforting but that we found stifling, suffocating, at best. At worst, we knew that the blanket could be removed at any time and we would be left shivering in the dark.

As a whole, my parents ruled with a kind of benign neglect. A benign neglect, punctuated by the times when Mother, in particular, was so present she was as overwhelming as The Great and Powerful Oz, controlling us all behind the curtain while we were as unaware as Dorothy and her gang that there was even a control board.

Even at tender ages, we were let loose in the early morning, with no need to check in. We traveled fairly far afield, with the only rule that we had to return home when the street lights came on. And so, we were able, with some frequency, to absent ourselves from the toxicity that suffused the atmosphere in our beautiful house.

On any of those beautiful and free days, I would leave the house with my pocket money and meet up with Pam at the top of my street. From there we would walk to the new shopping center and spend hours between the bookstore and the five-and-dime, trying to figure out whether we wished to spend our allowances on candy buttons or Superman comics. When I was a little older, Pam and I would take our bicycles and peddle a circumference around town: Downtown, to the drive-in, the swimming pool, the shopping center, through neighborhoods of brick ranch houses spaced as precisely as the candy dots we would peel from the white paper and eat as carefully as though they were magic pills, each one granting us just one wish. Pam always wanted to wish for more wishes, infinite wishes, but I parceled my wishes out carefully: I wished for beauty; I wished not to wear glasses; I wished to be the same as everyone else; I wished for a normal mother.

A friend once told me, "My sister-in-law gave birth to illnesses instead of children." I think about that in conjunction with my mother a lot because Mother was a woman who gave birth to both simultaneously. In her manic phases, Mother had an endless store of energy that allowed her to handle her mental illness and her babies at the same time, if with little facility. When she was depressed, which was more of the time, she didn't handle either.

Mother had, from birth, a disposition toward unhappiness that could not be undone. I learned this much later from her writing and from stories Hannah told me. One went like this: When Mother was a little girl, her father used to brush the tangles from her long, unruly hair by bribing her with small peppermints. Each time she did not yell when a snarl was yanked, she received one of the small pastel candies; each time she complained, one was taken away. She was not allowed to eat the candy until her hair was brushed and plaited. Sometimes Mother had a handful of mints to eat, sometimes she had none. Mother's parents were always trying to tame her or to stop her from her tantrums. Apparently, Mother's tantrums were so frightening that their parents would do anything to stop them. My bubbe and my zayde pampered and petted Mother, walked a wide berth around her as though she were a Ming vase they were worried would shatter.

But the lesson Mother learned from the mints and the promises was the weird art of give and take with strings always attached; and that is what she practiced on us. Even if there were no mints to mark her behavior, Mother's tantrums never ceased, and she continued to expect others to put up with them.

9.

In our forties, my sisters and I began to plan a trip together each year. Friends who did not get along with their sisters were aghast at spending that much time alone with siblings; friends who did were envious. Despite how close in age we were—there were only four years between the three of us—or maybe because of it, my sisters and I did not spend a lot of time together as children unless we were forced. Mother liked to devise ways to force us. She favored board games and decks of cards over dolls and other toys because she thought it might keep all three of us out of her hair at once. She encouraged us in games of Masterpiece and Operation, which led not to sweet and fun play but to intense competition and squabbling, sometimes ending in real physical fighting. I was, and still am, both a terrible loser and a gloating winner. When I got annoyed at losing or if I was winning too much, Sara would suddenly leave the game. Erika would insist we play over and over again until everyone had won a time or two. We thought her mad.

We were close in age but quite obviously nothing alike in temperament—I was introspective but fairly socially adept; Sara was quiet, serious and a loner; Erika wanted to make everyone happy. Mother simply wished we would get along with each other and leave her be. As we grew older, Mother insisted I take Sara along with me when I met my girlfriends, not caring about my protestations that I didn't want my sister along nor Sara's that she didn't wish to go with me. When we were coerced, no one had a good time. Sara sulked in a corner, and I apologized for my sister's weird behavior.

There was always a palpable aura of violence in the house, fueled by Mother's rages and Father's threats, and the three of us picked up the anger and ran with it. I stuck a fork in Sara's back; she "accidentally" hit me in the eye with one of my father's golf clubs when he was trying to teach us how to putt on our back lawn. Sara still has a scar bisecting her left eyebrow from when Erika and I chased her around the house and she tried to escape by sliding under the metal bed frame in her room. Our bizarre games usually ended with someone getting hurt.

Although we were never actually hit by our parents, they were famous for their intimidation. Father always said he would give us something to cry about whenever we whined or moaned about anything. We never knew when to take him seriously: His style was to make a joke out of everything, even our misbehaviors. We were nourished on his cruel sense of humor early and learned to take little of what he said seriously. Mother, who took every infraction of ours, of his, absolutely seriously, watched our father tease us, angry, but she did nothing about it. Her own favorite promise was that she would rip out one of our arms and beat us with its bloody stump.

There was much yelling and screaming, all of it over-ridden by the omnipresent feeling of our own powerlessness. Sara repeatedly tried to run away, the first time at age five. After packing a suitcase that contained one of my shoes, Sara headed down the driveway with me following. We were so loud in our disagreement that Mother heard us and put an end to Sara's journey. Who knows how far Sara would have gotten if we had not made so much noise; Mother would not have heard us above the cacophony of her own mind.

Of our sisters' trips Mother said, jealously, "I wish you would take me along." But that was just the point, we didn't want her along. We had traveled with her. We understood how difficult it was. We did however always take Mother with us, and our father, too, in the stories we told.

We clung to the things that made us feel connected and ignored all that had separated us. We thought we were being honest. We told stories as if any one of them could be protection against what was to come. And the truth was, after both our parents fell so ill, those trips with each other were moments, tiny milliseconds, of bliss in the midst of the death and decay that surrounded us. We assumed we could make sense of it all, hashing and rehashing our pasts, cutting in, interrupting each other, dissenting as often as we agreed.

In the midst of it all, there was always the specter of our familial roles. There was always the knowledge that the way our parents had reacted to us and us to them would forever cast a shadow over our stories. In truth, it was entirely possible we all had different childhoods, something we acknowledged but did not dwell upon. We made jokes about how we were or were not like our mother or father, about which of us was the favorite, which the outcast. Although we were still relatively young, we began to examine more closely our own mortality. And we always bought trip insurance in case we had to suddenly cut our time short and fly back to attend to death.

10.

Some people overcome incredible odds, horrible life-threatening, sanity-threatening events. I met a woman once who had lost three siblings in a house fire. Two others, including her twin brother, had died early in life. The mother, an unmedicated manic-depressive and alcoholic, somehow found the strength to go on, even thrive. My friend called her mother the hero of her life. I would have liked such an outcome for my own mother; I would have relished it. But even after everything—the breakdown, the divorce, the new house and job—her drinking, if lessened, did not stop. And long after my sisters and I had forged lives of our own, she made her angry presence felt. The years until the final diagnosis were more cruel than anything I had felt from her as a child.

Within a year or two after she retired from her job, whatever ground she had gained receded under her feet. She was lonely again, and needy. She complained of pain everywhere, and her drinking began to take control of her. For the next ten years, she seemed more and more despondent, angry, cruel. There was nothing to talk with her about other than what bad things had happened in the world that day, which of her friends had died, what part of her body hurt. It was as if the fifteen years she spent in the work world had never happened. Friends and coworkers fell away.

As much as she behaved otherwise Mother convinced herself that she was unimportant, that no one was paying attention. I wonder now, was Mother so starved for attention, so hungry for it that she could never get filled? No matter how many mints were given, no matter how much food was cooked and served, no matter how many times her parents apologized for the lack of food at her wedding, none of it was enough to fill her up. Or get even close. She spent the rest of her conscious life trying to get people to pay attention to her. And they did. They did. But I wish I'd had the strength to tell her that people tired of listening to her because chronic unhappiness is so damned boring, and the listener is ill-equipped to help—they are helpless. That is why therapists get paid to listen to people's angst.

While Mother's overriding complaint was that no one ever really paid attention, no one listened to her, I knew that all I did was listen. I heard every word she said. I have the scars to prove it.

There is an old Jewish tale of a man who meets a wolf on the road, escapes from danger and goes about telling the townspeople of his meeting and escape. Farther down the road, he comes upon a lion and once again evades its clutches and lives to brag about it, forgetting about the wolf. And finally, he meets a snake with poisoned fangs and manages to emerge unscathed, all the while boasting of that escape and neglecting to mention the earlier dangers. Such it is with the Jewish people: New dangers can make them forget the old ones.

Sara said to me, as we read through some of Mother's journals one evening, "Perhaps it is a good thing that Mother has lost her mind. That way," she smiled, "she will never be able to remember how truly unhappy she was."

I have spent far too much time and energy, years and years of it, trying to parse, to dissect, Mother's moods. For so much of my life, I thought that if I could just figure her out, I would be able to let her go. But her despair was so large and so overwhelming that no matter where she was it consumed all the oxygen in every room. I could not let go of her. In the end, she left me when her mind ended and no smidgen of my relationship with her was left.

The Reciting of the Prayers for the Dead: The Kaddish

> "*What came is gone forever*
> *every time—*
> *That's good! That leaves it open for no regret—no fear radiators,*
> *lacklove, torture even / toothache in the end—*
> *Though while it comes it is a lion that eats the soul—and the*
> *lamb, the soul, in us, alas, / offering itself in sacrific to change's*
> *fierce hunger—hair and teeth—and the roar of / bonepain,*
> *skull bare, break rib, rot-skin, braintricked Implacability.*
> *Ai! ai! we do worse! We are in a fix! And you're out, Death let*
> *you out, Death had the Mercy, / you're done with your*
> *century, done with God, done with the path thru it—Done*
> *with / yourself at last—Pure...*"
>
> —Allen Ginsberg, "Kaddish Part I"

1.

"May there be much peace from heaven and good life and satiety and salvation and comfort and saving and healing and redemption and forgiveness and atonement and relief and deliverance."
—*The Kaddish*

The rules of the Kaddish state that it can only be recited in the presence of a minyan—ten adult Jews—which is why during the seven days of Shivah, people gather in the house of mourning. To make sure there is a minyan. To make sure no one in such grief is alone. No one can withdraw into their own world at such a time for it is not a time to be alone. I didn't know, until I was first confronted with it at my father's death, that no where in the Kaddish is there talk of death. Nowhere are there words that describe those who have passed. Prayers leading up to the Kaddish talk about those who are gone but the Kaddish itself is a prayer affirming God, a prayer we must say with others: We may be born alone and we may die alone, but we are not meant to mourn that way. The Kaddish brings us together at the exact moment we begin to fall apart.

When I got the news about Mother, I was grateful to hear it in the company of Hannah and my sisters. I was grateful to have them as part of my minyan. For most people, life unravels bit by bit until they are at the end of the skein. The unraveling of Mother was rushed by chance or destiny or biology or all of those, so that the whole ball of yarn of her was let loose at once. It comforted me not to have to look at that empty reel alone.

I read about beta-amyloid and plaques in the brain and how, according to *The New York Times,* a radioactive dye could perhaps find it, perhaps lead to an early diagnosis. But if I could know, would I want to know? Would I want to see it coming? I was recently in a car accident and I could still see the car coming at mine in that moment before impact. Wouldn't it feel like that? Wouldn't I be terrified in my helplessness? Wouldn't each minor, tiny memory slip, every moment of normal forgetfulness frighten me even more? Because each slip, each lost moment would pile up upon the other.

Many of the articles tried to be upbeat, cautioned against panic, argued one could lead a life, circumscribed for sure, but still a life. But what kind of life?

How soon would it be until names slipped away, until faces began to disappear, until the ordinary moments of life—bathing, personal care, eating, the tiny pleasures—became things another person had to take care of? To be alive and not alive.

How do you prepare yourself for the loss of yourself: hoard pills, read manuals from the Hemlock Society? And then if you know you are ready to jump, to make that final leap, when push comes to shove, how will you know when it is time to consciously say good-bye before you can no longer say it? In some moment of clarity, before the disease progressed too much, would I be able to take my own life? And if I did would it be cowardice or bravery?

When Mother said "Shit, shit, shit," and burst into tears at the initial diagnosis, had there been a second, an instant's hesitation when she thought about taking her own life? If so, I didn't see it. She never mentioned suicide to any of us. And as far as we knew, at no other time in her darkest depressive moments had she thought about taking her own life. Even when she shut down during her breakdown, she still allowed herself to be saved. As depressed as she had been for so many of her years, she still held on as fast to life as a drowning man to a life raft.

I could not imagine following the path of my mother and her mother before her. I could not imagine living as Mother did, even with the small joys that life afforded her, and I certainly could not imagine experiencing the full mental decline I bore witness to. Or rather, I could imagine it: People taking care of me, washing and dressing me, *seeing* me when I had no idea I was even being seen or taken care of. I obsessed about it. It felt like a horror movie. Like watching naïve heroes approach the door they should not open. Stop. Do not enter.

    Mother had seen her own mother slide into the abyss and yet Mother seemed to have no sense of her own slide, no single moment of awareness that she was following the same path. More than a year after she moved into *Menuchat Lev*, we sat on her bed watching television together. When a commercial about a man with Alzheimer's came on, Mother turned and said to me, "How sad for that poor man. How very sad."

Hannah called me every couple of weeks and after conversation about the other things in our lives, she would always say, "Every time I think about your mother I just cry. I can't stand to think about her this way."

    I told Hannah honestly that I wasn't as sad for her at this point as I was for us. The queen was dead, but the ladies were still waiting. The first few years, it was hard for Hannah to hear a word against her older sister, no matter the pushes and pulls of their relationship. But as the years passed and Mother flew faster and faster on the downward slope, watching Mother lose herself by the day wore Hannah out.

    Our conversations over the years were often circular,

SHIVAH

spiraling around Mother and who she was, who she had been, and then tightening into the way all of us expressed our peculiar grief. Hannah continued to mourn the loss of her sister while I just threw myself into doing things: coming for visits, dealing with her doctors, Mother's medicines, sitting with her for hours just holding her hand. My actions kept the goblins away.

2.

Krenk: A sickness that manifests itself differently in each generation, sickness as a changeling.
A farshlepteh krenk: A sickness that hangs on and on.

In addition to the looming threat of Alzheimer's there was also, I learned years ago, a history of sadness and madness that ran matrilineally on both sides of my family: melancholy, madness, attempts at suicide, despair, depression, postpartum psychosis.

My great-grandmother spent her entire life alternating between talking to God and trying to commit suicide. She brought her tuberculosis with her to the United States, knotted in her chest like the bread and garlic knotted in a napkin attached to her skirt, and when she was finally allowed to leave Ellis Island, both the disease and an incipient madness completely took hold.

Before she left the old country, she tried to hang herself with a bathrobe belt thrown over the bedroom door; she threw herself down the stairs when her periods did not come; angry, she chose to endure days and nights of agony from doses of emetic that rid her of everything but my grandmother stubbornly clinging to her insides. In America, my grandfather had to cut his mother-in-law down from where she had tried to hang herself again, this time with a rope in the attic. Another time, my grandmother pulled her mother away from being run over by a subway train. And still another time, my bubbe found her mother in a bathtub full of water with an empty bottle of gin. My great-grandmother was persistent if inept. My bubbe kept trying to tell the Angel of Death that there was no one at home but he wasn't listening.

And who could blame my great-grandmother's suicide attempts after all? They weren't her fault: Her past hung around her neck like an albatross. My great-grandmother came from Galicia, a piece of land between the old Russia and Poland, carved out of Ukraine. All records are lost, borders have been redrawn, and whole towns and villages have disappeared. Only lately have I even seen the area parsed by scholars.

My great-grandmother refused to remember anything, and she didn't like to talk about the old country at all. She refused, even in moments of clarity, to tell her story, although I do know that her mother was raped and tortured and blinded in one eye by Cossacks. Frightened more for the life of her young baby than for herself, she buried my great-grandmother in shallow earth to hide her, to keep her safe, leaving only a small air hole for the baby to breathe.

My great-grandmother was eighteen months old when she was buried alive, when she lay listening to the pain of her mother's rape, saw first-hand the blood that dripped from her mother's lost eye, lanced by a blade.

My great-grandmother arrived in America, twenty years later, an uneducated peasant, still traumatized, with my grandmother in her arms and another baby in her belly. She was illiterate, uneducated, dirt poor. Her only suitcase was stolen on the docks while she waited for her husband, who had arrived months earlier, to meet her. What remained in her travel bag was a silver samovar and a gold-plated locket, both of which I now own. That was all the finery she had. When my grandmother was thirteen, she was sent to a lawyer's office to obtain a divorce for her parents.

My great-grandmother's life was a ruin from beginning to end but God laughed at her attempts to die, and she lived to be eighty-eight. When I first knew her, she was already an old, stout woman who lived with five other old women in a large yellow house, shabby but comfortable, by a lake in upstate Massachusetts. The lake had leeches, and when we swam in it, we came out covered in them. She had long, yellow-white hair that she braided around her head and a large, round face creased with the web of lines that her daughter and granddaughter would later inherit, the skin fragile as worn lace.

In the few short years we knew my great-grandmother,

my sisters and I were never comfortable with her. She tried to hug our thin bodies to her big fat breasts; she called us *shayna punims*. She scared us with her bulk, her perpetual frown, the foreign language that sounded like she was coughing up something from deep in her throat.

Later, after she went into a nursing home, we visited her, and still she frightened us. Fat as Jabba the Hut, she sat in a chair, her legs wide in her cotton printed dress, her stockings rolled down around the ankles of her laced oxfords. She muttered curses. Her favorite was *Vocks vie ein a tisbela*, which loosely translates: May you grow like an onion with your head in the ground and your feet up in the air. *Fuck you*, Mother said years later, had nothing of the power of that curse. My poor, poor great-grandmother. Who could fathom what she had wanted for herself? She had never even been allowed to dream, to want, to wish; she was too busy just surviving. Or, rather, trying *not* to survive.

I will never know if my great-grandmother's unhappiness was born to her or given to her in that shallow grave in which she was placed. The stories I asked for came too late to be checked for accuracy. I do know that whatever hope she came to America with was stolen from her with her only suitcase.

In the few fuzzy black and white photographs that survived, she appeared a woman under fifty, her demeanor stern, her face set hard, her body thick and forbidding. There was no recorded moment of the doe-like youthful beauty that her daughter, my grandmother, had possessed before her life also wore her down like an old eraser. There was certainly no hint in my great-grandmother's face of the arresting beauty of my mother. My mother told me she once saw a photograph that my great-grandmother brought with her from the old country and in it she saw her own face, but the photo was long lost. It was fitting. Mother's legacy of beauty and madness had to start somewhere.

Years later I would gaze at the one photograph I had of her—so stern, so solemn, surrounded by her two children—and feel a strong kinship. I may not have been actually buried alive, but I knew how it felt to be suffocated by your mother. I knew what it was like when protection turned into destruction.

3.

Everyone at the nursing home where my grandmother spent the last fifteen years of her life thought she was "the best." They all called her Bubbe. She was everyone's granny. "Bubbe is just the sweetest thing!" the nurses would gather around to say whenever we came to visit. "So easy, so lovely! We all adore her around here."

Even when Bubbe became incontinent, lost her false teeth, wandered along the halls like a specter, she was "the best." Mother cried so much when Bubbe died that I thought I was missing something. We had been preparing for her death for nearly two decades. Wasn't it good she was gone? My mother quoted an old Yiddish saying: "There is no bad mother and no good death."

I always resented the way my parents talked to each other or to their parents in Yiddish— a secret language to which none of us children were privy. I didn't push to be included or ask to learn it because, I think, there was a part of me that didn't really want to know their secrets. The few times I had snuck down the hall to eavesdrop on one of my parents' parties, I was rather disappointed. The people there were the people I saw every day except they'd all had too much to drink. When a friend asked me why I hadn't learned that ancestral language, I shrugged. It's hard to know what will be important to you later in life. To know which moments will change you without you even being aware.

A few years before Bubbe lost her own "remembers," as an old woman I knew used to describe dementia, I had her sit down and tell me her story. I didn't want any more memories lost to history. And this is what she told me. These are her own words:

> *I was born into poverty and my parents were first cousins and so my father decided to come to America, the land of milk and honey. Shortly after my birth, he left us with his parents in the old country, which my mother described as a living hell, and he came to Connecticut where he got a job in a factory. After ten months he sent for us. I came down with measles on the ship and we had to be quarantined, I don't know for how long and then our luggage was lost so we had nothing. We lived in a cold water, three-room flat and my father made six dollars a week, but*

SHIVAH

my father got sick and unable to work and then my mother became pregnant again. My mother was determined to move to Boston and so we packed up and did. Then my father took up with a bad crowd, drinkers, and he was a man who could not drink, and I was always sent to the bars to bring him home.

We lived in an attic flat over a barroom on Hampton Avenue and many days I had to step over drunks in the hallway, but our flat was clean and we tried to be like a family. I took care of my younger brother as my mother was sick with tuberculosis and malnutrition and had to be sent away. Then we had to split up. I went to live with an aunt and my brother went back to relatives in Hartford. My mother went to the hospital where she was given six months to live. My father? He just wandered around. Then, one day my father brought my little brother to the hospital and just left him there, said there was nowhere else for him to go. My mother was beside herself and so at age twelve I had to do something. I had heard that the town of Sharon, Massachusetts, was good for people with lung disease so I prevailed upon the doctor to release my mother into my care *and I found a small house in Sharon and talked the people there into letting me have it rent free for a month. I moved my mother and my brother and me there. I borrowed some money from an uncle, applied for welfare and found a house to buy for $800. I worked after school to support us. Then the house burned down. But by this time I had taken some business courses and had a decent job and with insurance on the house I bought another larger house and rented out rooms. My father came back and things went well for a while until my mother had a breakdown and had her first attempt at suicide and my father left again. I spent all my time with my mother taking her to doctors. She was in and out of hospitals. She kept trying to kill herself. She tried to throw herself in front of a train and she tried to drink a half gallon of chemicals. She was taken to Foxborough State Hospital.*

The house was rented through the summer but then in the winter the pipes burst and it was all too much to take care of and my brother did not want to live there so he went to Boston and went to work for Filene's.

SHIVAH

And then I met my husband and my prayers were answered for I had someone to share my troubles with.

I felt her simple and heartbreaking account left out a lot of the details, including the fact that she was pregnant with my mother when she married and including the fact that her young husband was one of six boys who doted on yet another difficult mother, a mother who never quite got over her son having to marry a woman she found beneath him. But that was as much of Bubbe's story as she thought was important. As soon as she married and had children, everything was fine. That was her big lie.

Pain for my grandmother, unlike her own mother, was something to be mentioned, only mentioned, in passing. The burden of caring for her constantly suicidal mother, of overlooking her handsome husband's many business failures, of an eldest daughter who came out of the womb somehow "different," all that disappeared. She fashioned a happy life for herself, with a happy past. Nothing had been too insurmountable for her to overcome, not the journey to America as a babe in arms, not the measles that kept her quarantined on the boat for two weeks, not the loss of all the family possessions. Not the poverty, the multiple moves to houses more humble than the last, not her pregnancies when she had no idea where her next meal was coming from, not her visits to welfare for clothes for her mother, not the fact that her father was an alcoholic and had to be fetched frequently from some bar, not even that she had to raise her younger brother because her mother could not. Not that she never finished high school and never became the lawyer she dreamed of. None of those things mattered. She had two beautiful daughters, grandchildren, a home to live in (paid for, unbeknownst to her, by her daughters as her husband had left almost no insurance), the sun was shining, life was good.

I acquiesced to her subterfuge. She could tell the story as she pleased. If she preferred a tale that read like a children's story where hope won out and desperation had no lasting effects, so be it.

4.

My mother wrote this about my bubbe:

> *My mother wrinkled early and had the habit, when sitting, of pressing one hand to either side of her face, tightening the skin so that she looked younger than I can ever remember her. I used to think it was a vanity thing, a futile exercise like those we practiced when we were very young, pressing pencils in our cheeks to make dimples, sleeping with the tips of our noses pulled up by tape.*
>
> *But it wasn't that at all. What she had been doing all those years was getting her head together. Or holding her head together.*
>
> *I remember what she went through, with a family of assorted dependent, demanding*

relatives, and that she did it all without liquor or Valium or consciousness raising or assertiveness training. Without affairs or becoming a lesbian, without marching and with very quiet protest and an ulcerated stomach and migraine headaches and chronic neck tension and the occasional prolonged weep.

And an ultimate rejection of all this was unbecoming, unpleasant, ugly.

And I wonder if her hands were really pressing up on her cheeks or covering her ears.

She catalogued a litany of the ills of her friends, but they were physical and not character defects or moral weaknesses or ethical impurities. Those who were not good were dismissed, refused, unrecognized. Marriages could be good if everyone tried harder (though definitions of "try" and "harder" were never given) and she would commiserate with your troubles but so that only you could solve them. By trying harder.

After my grandfather's death, my grandmother's next-door neighbor wanted to marry her. He had been in love with her for years. My grandfather had even kidded her about it. She was still lovely then, with her long, white hair braided and wrapped into a knot on her head, just as her own mother had worn it. Her clear, hazel eyes, her skin as yet unlined with the wrinkles that would soon crisscross her face like writhing snakes. At sixty, she had a plump and girlish figure, and she used those youthful good looks to encourage the man who was in love with her to fix her screens, mend her fence, help her in the garden, get her milk when he ran to the store. But marriage? She knew what that meant.

When children were no longer in the picture, what was the point? Someone to fix meals for, someone to snore beside her in the double bed in which her husband had spent his last hours? No thank you. She once told me that the benefit of being a widow was that she was done with "all that." I was old enough to know exactly what she meant, but sorry she felt that way. My grandfather was a handsome, virile man and he adored her. She coped with being an orphan and a widow by sitting for her real estate license. She refused all marriage proposals, cut her hair short and went to work.

Gathering the bits of my past was illuminating and disconcerting. The fact that Bubbe's parents were first cousins could explain both the melancholy and the madness. The madness that drove my great-grandmother helped me understand Bubbe's desire to rewrite her own history to make it more palatable. And I understood her reluctance to recognize a similar disease in her own daughter. I got that she needed to soothe, to smooth her own past and to see only the good in others. I had sympathy for her own particular madness: The madness of forgetting everything bad before she forgot everything.

Then, in a packet of old photos and papers that my father was going to toss out when he and his wife moved into a new house, I found an oral history of his mother, my other grandmother, with a penciled postscript that she must have written shortly before she died at the age of ninety-nine. It stated that her own mother had not died of tuberculosis like she told everyone. My paternal great-grandmother had not, at least not directly, succumbed to some physical illness as my father and his own sisters had been led to believe. As everyone *knew*. In her twenties, after the birth of her seventh child, my paternal great-grandmother was sent to the hospital where she wasted away, a dozen years later, from "melancholy." My grandmother had found it necessary, finally, at the end of her life to tell the truth.

We knew that most of the children had been farmed out to neighbors until my grandmother, at twelve, was allowed to bring them home and care for them. We knew she then raised her brothers and sisters and took care of her own father for the rest of his life. We knew she was widowed young, had no more than a seventh-grade education, and was taken care of by my father and his sisters for all her widowhood. We knew she was a tough old bird who thought whining and complaining about anything was a waste of time. But we didn't know the most important thing: Her mother left her and her brothers and sisters. She abandoned them and went to a hospital to die of a deep and profound sadness that was then untreatable. And my grandmother was ashamed to tell anyone about it.

The "melancholy" that afflicted both my great-grandmothers, that tore apart their lives, the illness that had claimed Mother long before she succumbed to Alzheimer's, was in our genes. We were time bombs waiting to go off. Or perhaps we already had: Both Sara and I suffered from bouts of depression; I was in therapy on and off for years; Sara took medications although I have no idea which ones; Erika dealt with her own moodiness by ignoring it—she took a page from Bubbe. But I had to wonder: Were the same genes that carried sadness related somehow to the loss of the women's faculties? Were those same genes ours?

There was extraordinary longevity in the women on both sides of my family: Ninety-nine, eighty-eight, ninety-two. Mother, at eighty was physically healthy. But what good was it to live a long, long life if one was bound on one side by sadness and the other by not knowing?

5.

An old Jewish lesson has it that a saint and sinner, both passengers on an ocean liner, were in the middle of storm and they feared the boat would sink. "Save us, Lord," cried the sinner. But the saint warned him to be quiet. "Don't let God know you are here," he said, "or it will be the end of us!"

I didn't want to be like Mother, a woman for whom no amount of goodness from others, no outpouring of love from friends and family, no snippets of kindness from strangers, or favors done for no reason, could ever reach completely to the depths of the unfathomable bottom of her soul. She had sought peace, for years in her summers by the water, then alone in her doll house, but it always escaped her. I needed, *wanted*, to feel grateful for the peace and happiness I had found. I needed, *wanted* not to dwell on what had not transpired or even what had been lost.

If there were days still, and always would be, when my childhood felt like an amputated limb, when the pain ghosted itself in my heart, I wanted, needed, to say my prayers for that dead time, those dead moments, my past life, and move on. The Kaddish is not about death or mourning, rending clothes or tearing hair; it is about praising God and being glad of him. It is a sad wail of a prayer that says: I am still here and I know what is expected of me.

I might have wondered whether my family wasn't doubly cursed with both the *krenk* and the forgetting—who wouldn't want to forget, consciously or not, a history like ours?—but on most days, even if my one blessing consisted of just waking up, I went with it. I made myself feel lucky. I knew that the cynical veneer I often presented was just that, a shell: Deep down where it counted, I was an optimist. I didn't wish to forget that. I did not wish to forget anything. I welcomed the phantom pain. Because despite everything— the *krenk* and all its accompanying symptoms, the looming specter of losing my self like my mother and grandmother before me, the pain of failing at my marriage, of all the empty years of my childhood—I had been born into a relative fortune. My bubbe would admonish me, "When you are feeling sorry for yourself for having no shoes, think of the man who has no feet." She was right.

But I also knew I shouldn't get too cocky about good fortune: I could catch the interest of the devil or his minions—*ayen hora*, the evil eye who lurks around every corner. I learned that from my bubbe, too. If you are too proud of what you have, the demons will control you. They are just waiting to make a move when good calls attention to itself.

I was very concerned that my gratefulness at all the good in my life would somehow do me in. I wonder still: How do you count your blessings, how do you praise God, without daring the *ayen hora*?

Early Jewish literature just accepts the idea of the presence of evil as fact, precluding any explanation of it or any discussion of its origin. But post-Talmudic explanations say that the evil eye contains the element of fire and so spreads destruction. The angry glance of a man's eye calls into being an evil angel who takes vengeance. All measures taken against *ayen hora* are either preventative or counteractive: Successful men, beautiful women and newborn babies are more likely to attract the attention of the evil eye. So you try to disguise both beauty and riches. If you brag too much you must immediately spit; the ugliness of that act dissipates your prideful words. If you sigh with relief that something bad hasn't happened, you must knock wood three times because odd numbers repel demons while even numbers attract them.

But my mother never seemed worried that bemoaning her life and her fate, the promising future she had left behind, would tempt the evil eye. She never seemed worried that all her railing against her existence might help God to turn away from her. How could she have been so careless with both her curses and her wishes? Did she have no faith left? Later I would learn from her writings that she had been witness to a fallen angel first hand when she wrote about her affair with the love of her life and the final hours when they made love by the light of a *yahrzeit* candle burning on his bedside, a candle of whose significance my mother's lover had known nothing, but in whose almost extinguished light she saw the end of the only happiness she ever had. Because the candle, which stays lit for twenty-four hours, had been burning well before her arrival that last evening.

All the old women in my family are long dead and soon my mother would join them and I would, like her, place stones on her grave because the Talmud tells us that the body is the shoe of the soul. It is only the holder of what is most important, and so, when we mourn, we are meant to put a stone in our shoe to remind us. And when we visit the graves of the dead, we are meant to leave a small stone behind as proof that we were there. Perhaps it is even possible that the person lying beneath that stone feels its weight.

The Examination of the Souls of Those Still Living

How are we worthy of still being alive?

> *"And who by fire*
> *Who by water*
> *Who in the sunshine*
> *Who in the night time*
> *Who by high ordeal [. . .]*
> *And who shall I say is calling?"*
> *—Leonard Cohen, "Who by Fire"*

1.

As we prepared for Mother's eightieth birthday the third summer after her diagnosis, my sisters and I argued over the venue, the time, the kind of celebration. It wasn't to be too fussy, we all agreed. But I decided I needed to make a cake. I couldn't remember if I had ever made a birthday cake for Mother or why it seemed so necessary that year: Mother would have been fine with one bought at the market. She would have been fine with a piece of chocolate or a cookie. I myself had a bad history with birthday cakes. I only remembered a couple of them as a child and my whole married life I hadn't had one unless I made it myself. I remember Ivy, at twelve, the last year of my marriage to her father, appalled that I didn't have a birthday cake. She had just noticed. So I felt compelled to make Mother a homemade one. In the familial favorite flavor: Coconut. My love language has always been food.

At first, we wanted to have the gathering at an elegant resort in the town of Chatham, on Cape Cod, where we could rent rooms and be self-contained for a week, where Mother could sit by the ocean and where we could quickly walk into town and *schmie* around the shops. It would be an easy drive for Sam and Hannah, and perhaps even Hannah's children and grandchildren and great-grandchildren would be able to attend. A few of Mother's friends could even make the trip. But it turned out the times didn't work out, and the inn was problematic: The rooms had to be rented for a full week. The cost was prohibitive.

Next, Erika proposed the island. I knew what that would entail. Erika would be at her own house there and the care of Mother would fall mainly to me. When Sara and I discussed the change, I said, "What right does Erika have to tell us when we should or should not spend time with Mother? That's why she wanted us here and not someplace else."

"She does see her more often than we do," Sara shrugged.

"That's geography. You know we offered to have her down near where we are and Mother refused. And besides Erika sees her out of guilt not love."

"That's not your place to say," Sara said fiercely.

"Maybe not," I said. "But it's true. And it isn't her place to decide when and where I need to see Mother."

"You don't always have to say everything that's true, you know."

The thing was that I *did* always have to say everything that was true; it was the only way I could ensure my own narration was accurate. I spent too much of my past dissembling or even ignoring what had been going on around me, and it was time to stop. I no longer wished to pretend that there was anything normal about us, about Mother, about anything. And I needed to confront my discomfort with Mother's new personality, with the ways in which it had changed all three of us.

Years ago, on my fortieth birthday I gave myself a present. I vowed to simply tell the truth, to live as much with integrity as I could. I slip occasionally, of course. I still keep my mouth shut when I want to shout. And if people won't let me always be truthful with them, at least I can try and be honest with myself.

What also became true was that in the next dozen years I would fly up and visit Mother five times a year. I would go to each place she lived: Assisted living, the memory unit, the hospital and finally the nursing home, and I would pull up a chair beside my mother, and I would stroke her arm and I would run my fingers over her balding head for hours each day for a week. I realized later there was guilt along with love, too, duty along with generosity, responsibility being the most complex of feelings.

When I spoke with Erika, I told her there was no way that Paul and I could stay in the tiny beach house with Mother for a week again. And where would Ivy stay? Sara? Sam and Hannah? Erika said she would figure it out. And she did. She found a larger rental that accommodated all of us. Sara, Ivy, Paul, Mother and I would be there for a week and there were extra rooms for others if they stayed a night or two. Even Father and his wife, Alice, planned to come to the island for a night or two.

It was settled. Not that the venue mattered. Mother's affection for the sea had always been a wild mix of desire and disappointment. Before her allotted weeks each summer, when she had gone to Cape Cod and then to the island, Mother built up expectations so huge they could never be accomplished: She would write, reams; she would meditate; she would get her act together; she would meet interesting people, fall in love, find inner peace. None of this happened. What she did do was walk and walk, like the French lieutenant's woman, solitary, along the beach. She drank and drank, again often alone. She stared at her typewriter for hours, rewriting the same paragraph, crumpling paper into bits as though someone were filming her. And then she would write reams and reams about why she wasn't able to write, how nothing came to her, how the day was cold or hot or gloomy or even wonderful. Everything was to blame but herself. I always wondered why she went out of her way to repeat experiences that always made her unhappy. Or, for that matter, why I helped facilitate such journeys, why I was doing so for the third year. Was I really expecting a good outcome?

And that third summer after her diagnosis, the summer of the party, Mother was even more fragile. We were all worried. Would Mother be too disoriented leaving *Menuchat Lev*? Would the party even mean anything to her? How would we manage everything? The past two summers I had made it through, shepherding Mother through the supermarket while I bought what I needed to take to the island, but there was too much to buy this year, for too many people. Just getting Mother on the ferry to the island would be difficult.

But things began to fall into place. Erika told me to give her a list of the groceries I needed and they would be shipped over and there when we arrived. Sara would go up a couple of days in advance and unpack the groceries and set up the house.

Paul and Ivy and I drove up from Virginia, spent the night with Hannah, picked Mother up at *Menuchat Lev* the next day and caught the ferry. It was a new boat that year and they served wine—Mother asked me for money and when I gave it to her, she bought a glass. Upon arrival at the house, she immediately opened one of the big bottles we had ordered for the party. Sara and Erika were furious, but I only wondered if we would have anything left for the celebration. Paul shrugged his shoulders at me and steered Mother and her full wineglass out to the wide wooden porch. He sat with her while the rest of us unpacked.

The beginning of the week was especially chaotic. Mother stayed quietly inebriated, beginning her wine drinking at about eleven a.m. after several cups of black coffee, just as she had done years before. She kept wandering off the porch looking for the water and one of us had to follow her each time. When I sent Paul out to get her, Mother's old anger flared.

"I have been coming to this island for many years," she said. "Did you think I would get lost?"

"No, but *I* would if I did not have you to guide me," Paul said as he walked and walked with her until she tired.

She brought several books with her—some sort of vestigial memory, perhaps—but we knew she could not read them. None of us got much reading done. By the time nightfall came and dinner was over and the dishes were washed, we were all exhausted. We decided it would be better to take shifts so that each of us could have some downtime.

Surprisingly Mother seemed stronger physically than she did the summer before. She often refused to ride in the golf cart and insisted on walking most places. She did not stumble and was not unsteady on her feet. But for most of the week, Mother chose to rock gently on the porch swing. Sara or I would sit with her, and she would clutch one of our hands in her own, but she would not say a word. She would just gaze out at the ocean for hours.

Sara and I tried to make simple meals on the old grill that came with the house, but as usual, Mother pushed her food around on her plate and gazed vaguely around for more wine; she never had an empty glass. Paul and Ivy both attempted to engage Mother in conversation so that I could get a break or go to the grocery or just sit alone. But while

Mother seemed glad to have any kind of company, even if she was silent much of the time, if our attention wandered from her, she grew agitated.

The island weather was iffy the first few days, but on one day that turned out particularly sunny, I walked with Mother down to the beach and we spread towels on the sand and sat for a while, and we then walked along the rocks, picking up what few shells had survived the pickings of the tourists in June and July.

Erika made a couple of brief appearances, but she was readying for a vacation with her husband and she seemed to have her hands full of other things to do. I talked with Sara about this. Actually, I complained. Erika seemed absent even when she was around. She was distracted and edgy. And even though she spent a little time at the house with Mother, in the main, she once again left the caretaking to me.

When I questioned her, Erika said, "I thought this would be a good time for you two to spend time with Mother."

I was furious and said so. "That wasn't the idea. The idea was that we would all be together and we would all help care for Mother."

Erika didn't want to talk any more about it. Instead, she said, "Let's not fight."

2.

Rousseau believes that children have a right to happiness; their liberty belongs to them. But Mother never believed in that notion. She believed in her own happiness and complained frequently that it had been co-opted by her children. And yet she had no issue with co-opting the happiness of us years later.

The truth? We were raised so very far from even the possibility of happiness. And I could not try to exit my life like my great-grandmother did: I had neither her cowardice nor her bravery. I could not go back and rewrite my life and make it pretty and peaceful like my grandmother did. And I could not try and obliterate it as my mother did. The most and the least I could do was try and dissect it. First, though, I had to understand that my own life had been built on things that were not in the least rational; however, my reactions to those things had to be.

I was well aware that there would be no last-minute rapprochement with either of my parents before their literal or figurative deaths. There would be no happiness in and of itself for any of us. I had to wring every ounce of liberty from my past and push it along and take it with me into the present.

My relationship with Mother had come as full circle as it ever would and ultimately it wouldn't matter what had or had not been said. I recognized that the difference between being an emotional orphan and a real one was slim. A quote in a book by philosopher Susan Neiman hit me hard: "The past looks simpler just because it is over and done with in a way the present is not."

    I knew, as I sat with Mother on the beach that summer of her eightieth birthday, as we watched the seaweed roll in and out over the rocks, that week would be my last on that island.

3.

The arrival of my father and his wife to the island in the middle of our week there with Mother was not a coincidence. Erika had planned it that way. She wanted him to be there for her party. I thought it was weird, inappropriate even, but I didn't talk her out of it. And so, at Erika's instruction, I wandered up to my father's house to carry an invitation to Mother's party. As I headed up the steps to the deck, he leaned on his walker and waved, shaking the cord to his oxygen tank that stretched through the sliding glass door into the house.

"We're having an eightieth party for Mother, Friday," I said. "If you and Alice would like to come for cake, we would love to have you. Hannah and Sam are coming over on the ferry this morning."

"That's nice," he said.

Alice came out of the door. "Hi, Leah," she said. "What's up?"

"The girls are giving Rachel a party for her birthday,"

Father said. "Friday."

"Do you want to go?"

"Yeah," Father said.

"Ok," Alice said, and she went back inside.

I stood up. "I'm going to take the golf cart to get Sam and Hannah at the ferry."

"Okay," Father said.

"Need any help?" Sara asked. She had just walked up the steps.

"No, you stay here." I said and walked back down the hill and climbed up the wooden steps to our porch.

"I'm going to the ferry to pick up Sam and Hannah," I told Mother.

"Oh, are they coming? Why?"

"For your birthday, Mom."

"Oh, how lovely," Mother said.

I turned to Paul. "Will you be okay here?"

He laughed, "Just fine honey. Will you need any help?"

"When I get back." I leaned down to kiss him. "Thanks," I said and began to walk toward the golf cart. I turned and shouted back: "Didja see my cake?"

"Only a thousand times," Paul said.

"What can I do to help?" Hannah asked, later.

"Have you seen my cake?" I asked.

"Only a thousand times," Hannah said. "And it's still gorgeous."

In one of Mother's journals she wrote about my father like this:

Love song to a soon-to-be-ex husband

So you finally learned to feel, my dear.
To come down into the holes I have been poking in our lives all these years.
It is unpleasant down here sometimes and I don't really blame you
for
Not wanting to come.
Or look in.
Or even yell, hello down there, how are you doing?

She also wrote about him like this:

He was the last purist; he walked out of Alfie because Michael Caine was acting such a shit. He was the first male feminist because at parties he gravitated to the corner where the women huddled and seemed to find their conversation fascinating, their problems intense, their situations provocative. Theirs, not mine. What my role was then I'm not sure, but somewhere over the many years there has been a definite reversal; where he now wants Mommy, the touch (I want to be touched), the answers (do we have any milk, wheat germ? Do I like quiche? Where are my sweat socks?). And I have come to, and passed, the point of I don't care. It's true. I no longer pat, stroke, fondle . . . he talked me out of that years ago when he withdrew my hand in public (it embarrassed him, made him feel funny, like a little boy, when we held hands in public). I have withdrawn myself. We don't talk, communicate, argue. We co-exist, mark time, tread water, pass in the hall. His eyes beg for affection, my puppy dog: pat me, feed me, love me . . .

They loved each other forever and were supremely embarrassed about it.

A year after Mother's diagnosis, Erika insisted on taking Mother to see old friends in Knoxville. It had been five years since my parents had seen each other and it seemed likely that it would be the last time. Each of them had decayed so profoundly that I wondered if they could even recognize the other.

On the phone, later that week, after Mother and Erika had gone back home, my father said to me, "Your mother looks terrible."

Later, that week, when I talked to Mother, she said, "Oy, your father. He looks awful, that walker, and he's so frail!"

Some years later, when Mother was barely verbal, living in the memory unit of *Menuchat Lev*, she asked the woman at the front desk for a telephone and called my father on his birthday. He was surprised. I was dumbfounded. How did she remember that when so many memories were lost? Was she even aware of what had happened to her mind?

4.

"Oh, your father's here!" Mother said with delight as she got up from the porch swing to put her arms around him. My father swayed slightly under the pressure and then said, "Happy Birthday, Rachel." He stepped back and looked at her. "You look good."

"I do not," she said, "and neither do you." A tiny spark of her still remained. She almost preened at the compliment. She then leaned around him and said, almost graciously, "Hello Alice."

Mother sat down on the porch swing and patted the spot beside her. "Sit next to me, Max." Father obliged while Alice arranged the oxygen tank and cord. Then Alice sat down in a chair next to Sam and began to make small talk, clearly unnerved by Mother's proprietary air with her husband. My father's hand rested almost unconsciously on Mother's leg and hers on top of it. Even when she had no longer wanted to be married to my father, she was loathe to let him go to anyone else. There was an uneasiness in her rejection as if she had expected him to call her bluff when she told him to leave. Years after the divorce, when her faculties were still intact, whenever she would see him she would still run her hands through my father's hair, rub his neck, grasp his arm, lean into him flirtatiously as if to say: *You know I could have you back in a minute if I wanted to, don't you.* Father's long-time girlfriend Shelia had just laughed it off, but then Shelia hadn't married him. Alice had.

And Alice, Alice seethed, perhaps rightly so, whenever Mother tried to claim Father as her own. Alice had no idea she had married a man with so little desire for confrontation, even at the expense of the feelings of others. I had known that for years. I wondered if perhaps Alice could be more generous now. Her husband and his ex-wife were only imitations of their former selves; they were small, glowing old-fashioned bulbs that could be turned off as easily as on; they threw off very little light or heat. She had little to be jealous of.

Hannah and I fixed plates of sandwiches and sides and brought them out for everyone. Ivy and her cousin, Michael, made a big show of bringing out the gifts and arranging them at Mother's feet. "These are for you, Grandma."

"Later," I admonished, knowing it would do no good. For children, birthdays are about nothing more than the presents, but Mother and Father ignored the gifts and everyone else on the porch and still had their heads close together when Peter and Erika finally arrived. Erika was breathless.

"Sorry we are late," she said, then she looked at Mother and Father, having a tête-à-tête. She rolled her eyes. "What's up with *that*?"

Sara said, "I have no idea, but just let them be. They look like they're having a very good time."

"Alice doesn't."

"She's a big girl. She can take care of herself," I said.

Alice ate a tiny piece of cake and then left quietly. It was ten minutes before I noticed she was gone. Both Mother and Father ate large pieces and then Mother kept asking for another small sliver until she had eaten at least two more pieces.

Mother seemed to love being the center of attention and opened her presents with childish glee: Two sweaters, a handbag, a photograph, a silver necklace, and a pair of earrings. Nothing she needed, all things I would have to remember to pack up for the return trip home, all things Mother quickly forgot completely about. All things I never saw again.

Father stayed the rest of the afternoon, sitting with Mother and not even shying away when she grabbed his hand. Then suddenly, around five, he said he was exhausted and asked Peter if he could take him home. Mother, with tears in her eyes, stood and hugged him and said, "When will I see you again, Max?"

Father shook his head and said, "I don't know, Rachel, I don't know." He leaned in and kissed her forehead. "Happy birthday, baby," and then, with Peter's help, he walked down the steps.

Mother looked down at her wineglass, which had been empty for some time. "Do you think someone could pour me a glass of wine?"

5.

That evening, Paul sat on the porch with Mother and smoked a cigar. He had offered to help me with the dishes but I was overloaded with people and I wanted, I needed, to be alone. I encouraged Sam and Hannah to take a walk. I let Sara help Erika take food back up to Erika's house and I pushed Michael and Ivy to go find kids their own age after an afternoon spent with all of us "old people."

I stood at the sink filling with water and remembered a sermon my rabbi had given a couple of months earlier in which he said that everything we do has the seeds of the sacred in it. If you do an act with intentionality, the task itself becomes sacred. It is not *what* you do, my rabbi said, but *how*. Look for the motivation, he said. Look deeper. Each of us has in us a spark of the divine.

As I scraped the food into the sink, I thought too about Thich Nhat Hanh who said when washing the dishes *wash the dishes*. Do not think of the tasks ahead, the things still left undone. Do not dream of the upcoming cup of tea when the dishes are finished. Do not dwell on whatever might come next. Be in the moment. Wash the dishes.

There was something divine in being in the moment. In acknowledging what was and being grateful for it. The past can confine you so that you cannot break its ropes and you drown like Houdini, tied in a glass cage, unable to be free. There is much freedom in letting go the past.

The Talmud teaches us that all of us are born knowing the secrets of the universe but before birth, we are touched by an angel above our lips and we forget. That indentation or fingerprint we see reminds us that it is our business to learn, to remember what we once knew and to know it again.

I looked out at Paul sitting with Mother and realized that almost four years had passed since the end of my marriage, since that moment when I realized that there was nothing I could do to resuscitate it. There had been many things that cracked the bond between Ben and me, and I tried my best to patch it with the glue of my will, until I shattered it irrevocably with my infidelity; but I had been aware, as I did it, that I was making that choice. I knew I was taking the coward's way out, but at the time it was the only way I had.

And from that moment, something in me changed. I began to learn how to find the profound in the ordinary. And in fact, I knew that without that belief in the sacred, there was no way I could have made it through the past few years. Without that intentionality, without that knowledge,

SHIVAH

without the ability to forgive Ben and myself for our failure, without just practicing basic forgiveness, essential forgiveness, I could never have gotten to the place in which I was standing. Washing the dishes from a party that was already gone from my mother's memory. Washing the dishes. Participating in the sacred. Being part of the divine. Washing the dishes.

6.

The last morning of that last summer week, I sat in one of the Adirondack chairs on the deck of Erika's house. It was six thirty in the morning. I looked out over the water and it was so clear and bright I could see Martha's Vineyard; it looked almost as if I could touch it. The water was nearly turquoise. The air was mild. I felt Erika's hands on my shoulders.

"Tea?"

"Sure."

She came back out carrying two steaming mugs.

"Are you hungry?"

"No, thanks."

"Where's Mom?"

I bit back the urge to tell her I had no idea, but instead I answered: "Still sleeping."

"Everyone else?"

"Still sleeping. I left a note."

"Even Sara?"

SHIVAH

"Yeah. Amazing, huh?" Sara was a notoriously early riser.

"Shall we go and get her for our walk? Do you think Paul can take care of Mother?"

"He'll make her coffee. They'll be fine."

"I'm sorry," Erika said suddenly.

I took a breath and said, as calmly as I could, "Why on earth did you plan a vacation to bump up against this trip? You've been frantic. We've hardly seen you. I thought this was supposed to be all three of us and the kids with Mom." I said these words, but I said them very calmly. Erika was very, very fragile.

She sat back in her chair. "I don't know. I just . . ."

I waited. I knew what was coming.

Erika burst into tears. Her selfishness was hard-fought, hard-won, but it never lasted very long. It was as if she longed to be selfish but just couldn't do it. She had instantly regretted The Letter to Mother, even though it wasn't selfish at all, even though it was an act of self-preservation. But after she sent it, Erika worried: Was it too harsh? Too long? Too tough? And then, when Mother didn't speak to her for six months, Erika was devastated, even though she acted like it was no big deal. Mother eventually relented, in her own peculiar way, and began to speak to her again, but she never treated Erika quite the same, never saw her again as the precious, perfect youngest daughter. Erika's letter was the final nail in the coffin Mother's ungrateful daughters had built for her.

And no matter how awful and abusive Mother had been, no matter how much she had taken advantage of Erika, Erika mourned that earlier relationship, as awful as it had been. But she would never admit that. So when Mother got sick, Erika went out of her way to once again play the dutiful daughter and take Mother to lunch once a week, buy her bras and underwear, take her shopping, act as a liaison with *Menuchat Lev*, making sure all the ducks were in a row. If she did all this out of a sense of misplaced guilt for writing The Letter too late, for getting years of stuff out of her system when it was far past time for doing it, I had to admit I was surprised she had written the letter at all. I told Erika, Sara told Erika: Just let it go. But Erika's emotions always ran perilously close to the surface and that would not change now. Erika would, like the rest of us, have to live with everything she had and had not done and just get on with it.

I sat and sipped my tea and watched my sister cry. "Are you done?"

Erika suddenly started to laugh. "I'm sorry I was such a bitch."

"Forgiven. Let's go get Sara and get on with our walk," I said.

The Statements of Comfort for Those Who Remain Behind

God is in the details.

1.

The winter after Mother's birthday celebration I got the idea to go up to Providence and bring Mother down with me to Virginia to stay several days. I proposed the plan to Hannah, Sara, and Erika. Hannah waffled. Sara thought it was incredibly stupid and that I would regret it. Erika, at first thought it a good idea, then after a disastrous Thanksgiving at her house, she decided that the trip should not be taken.

"Mother will drive you crazy," Erika said. "Don't do it. What is the point?"

I listened to her but then pressed Sara on why she thought it was such a bad idea.

"You know how Mother gets out of her element," Sara was vehement. "You saw her last summer. Even on the island that she loves so much. She wasn't good. She could hardly sit still. She had to have someone with her. Have you talked to Erika about Thanksgiving?"

I had. Erika went on and on. I listened. Apparently, Mother drank the whole time. At one point she had something in her glass and did not even know what it was. When Peter smelled it, even he could not tell. It worried all of them. Mother couldn't even help set the table. And then, after the weekend was over, when Hannah called her to ask her how it went, Mother went completely silent. She had no idea where she had been or what she had done.

I protested. "When I asked you about this last month you thought it was a good idea!"

"It seemed like one. I thought it would be."

"I don't care," I said. "The tickets are bought. I'm doing it."

The truth was I bought insurance on the tickets for a situation just like this, for the weather or for just in case. But still, I did not wish to cancel.

I called Hannah again.

"So, really, what do you think?"

Hannah still waffled. "It's up to you." Then she said, "Let me call her therapist. I'll call you back."

I sat down with Paul. "What do you think I should do?"

"Look," he said, "does it matter if she doesn't remember the trip after it happens?"

I thought about that. Did it? What was the point of it anyway? Wasn't the point just to give Mother a chance to spend some time with Ivy, with me, to see my new house, to get a chance to visit Sara's restaurant, get out of *Menuchat Lev* and have an adventure? If that was all it was, what difference did it make if the sensation only lasted for a moment? If the memory was even shorter than the trip?

"I guess not," I said. "You have a point."

"Think about why you are doing this," he said. "Who is it for?"

That was another good question, I thought. Who *was* the trip for? If it was for both of us, then both of us would have to be happy with the outcome. Could I be happy if Mother didn't remember the trip? Did it matter to Mother? If it was hard on Mother and she was disoriented and uneasy then it would not be a success. But, no matter how much it exhausted me, if Mother had a good time, then it would be worth it. So, was it worth the try, no matter how much Sara and Erika thought it a mistake? I decided yes. Ultimately, yes.

I was curious to hear what Hannah would learn from the therapist, but I could not think of a way to tell Mother that the trip I had told her about, the trip that she seemed so excited about, was off. Unless, of course, Mother didn't remember that I had told her about a trip in the first place. I knew it was a possibility but I could not bear the thought of that. In the end, the therapist was no help at all. Mother had not been to see her regularly in months. Hannah told me that all the therapist knew was that the doctors felt that Mother was "getting along fine" at *Menuchat Lev*, that everyone "loved" her, but that the progress of the disease was steady, and that the medicine, although they still gave it to her, would do little to slow the disease if she was still drinking and there was nothing the therapist could do about that as Mother was completely resistant to quitting. Other than that, Mother seemed to be managing as well as possible. Hannah told me that the therapist said the decision for the trip was mine alone; if I thought she could handle it, it was up to me. There was no reason to advise against it: As long as Mother was supervised carefully and not left alone, she was healthy enough to make the trip.

"So," Hannah said, "if you think you can handle it, go ahead."

"I can handle it," I said as I thought again about who the trip was for. Why I was doing it. What mattered about it. "That's not the point," I said.

2.

The Richmond airport was two hours away but it was the best airport to depart from because I could get a direct flight from there to Boston. Erika would pick me up in Boston and I would stay one night at her small mainland house near the city and then stay one night with Hannah in Providence. Erika, Mother, and I would all go out to lunch and then the next day Erika had arranged for a driver who would get me from Hannah's to Mother's and then drive the two of us to the Boston airport. I would drive with Mother the two hours home.

Coming back, we would be again picked up at the Boston airport by the driver and driven to Mother's, where I would drop her off and go to Hannah's, stay overnight with her and go back to the airport in the morning to catch a flight home. The plan seemed the least stressful. No change of planes, no airport transfers, no rides on subways or worries about parking and traffic. It was complicated but doable if I could keep Mother calm. Mother would spend three and a half days in Virginia with Paul, Ivy and me. I had planned enough activities to keep Mother busy and enough down time for the both of us. I hoped. Looking back on it, I think it was quite a mad idea. But at the time it all made perfect sense.

When I told Erika the plans were finalized, she said, "Buy some of that non-alcoholic Chardonnay and pour it into a bottle of the kind of wine she likes."

"Why didn't *you* do that? Why haven't *we* ever done that?"

"I don't know, but Sam told me about it. He's going to try it next time she is at their house. Try it."

"Will it work?"

"Who knows? Sam's been talking about it forever."

"But no one's ever done it?"

"Nope."

A few days before she flew up, I called Mother.

"Are you excited about the trip?"

"I am so excited I can hardly stand it," she said. "What do I need to do?"

"Nothing," I said. "It's all taken care of."

"What about my ticket?"

"Done."

"Wow."

"Just pick out some of the things you need and I will help you pack."

SHIVAH

"Oh, I can pack."

"Okay."

"I can't wait."

"Me, either, Mom."

"Now, give me the dates again."

And for the fifth time, I gave my mother the dates.

3.

Over the years I had imagined Mother's life as it could have been so many times that I felt finally glad to stop. The facts were laid out before me. She had Alzheimer's and she would get progressively worse; she would deteriorate at her own pace until she was gone in a whiff of smoke and ash and that would be it. Nothing else could happen then; all other possibilities were lost. I knew that imagination could be lethal if all one did was conjure up what *could* have been. There was no going back. There was no starting over. Any possibility of that had long ago been swept away by wine and disease and unhappiness and despair. And another disease more deadly than all of those had replaced it. All my sisters and I could do then was manage what was left.

I had my own life to recreate. I had a daughter for whom to imagine; I needed to help her shape a future. I needed to spend my time and energy on ways to make my own last years count—with hopeful, grateful imagery instead of regret and anger, useful rather than wishful. If the past was as graceless as it was arbitrary, so be it. If my heritage was madness and illness, at least I knew the truth and could do my best to maneuver around it.

God gave us free will, and we should exercise it. The evil eye is rooted in the universal pagan fear of a deity who begrudges man's perfect happiness. But who among us is happy, perfectly or even imperfectly, for more than moments at a time? It is a lot to expect: Happiness. Choose it, yes, but realize that it is not a permanent state.

A meditation before we say Kaddish says: "Birth is a beginning. Death a destination. But life is a journey." In between birth and death, with luck and God's good fortune, there is something called living. My mourning period was far too long. God would not have approved. He proscribed the length of mourning for a reason; He wished us to get on with our lives and do the job of living for those who were no longer able. Our task is to pick up the slack and do the work for those whose days have ended. No more rending of clothes, no more sack cloth and ashes. It was time to move on.

Here is what my mother gave me and what, for all the remaining days of my life, I will sit Shivah for:

- an unending delight at the sight of water
- an appreciation for the power of books and art and music
- an eye that decorates beautifully, that puts

disparate objects together to create a whole
- the talent to arrange flowers
- an ability to trust in and love my women friends
- a sense of adventure
- the will to live despite sorrow

These are the good things, these are the important things, and her loss has poked a hole in the ozone and it is up to me to try and fill it with beauty and appreciation and gratitude at the many blessings I possess.

Mother was a huge presence: She was a woman not to be trifled with, and as such, despite her madness and her anger and her illness, she left a big hole in the universe. Even if we may never be able to fill that hole, we must do the best we can to replace her in the world. It is our Biblical obligation to take over for her now that she can no longer perform her duties to God and the world. It is our duty to try.

The soul is always handicapped by the requirements of the body, and Mother's body, if still with her in flesh, had lost the piece of it that made it run properly. But I still have a fine if aging mind, I still have a body that works and as of now it houses a working mind. There is still much I can do. I need to keep busy and mind the gap.

There are no writings from Mother's last years. Whether it became too much for her to even try to write or whether putting her fears down on paper would make them real, or whether those lost notes were tossed into one of the seeming multitudes of black garbage bags that Erika and I tossed so casually onto the deck, we shall never know. But the pain of the writings I did find was more than I could bear. I am glad I did not find more.

In the next year, Ivy would go off to college in Boston, delighting Hannah, who would have another young girl to fill her house. Two years on, father would die and I would get through his eulogy as I would get through my Mother's eight years almost to the day later.

I had long ago said good-bye to both my parents. I had long ago made peace with my status as an orphan. My mourning was deep and grave. For both the parents who had tried to raise me.

My parents were careless, reckless people who crashed through the world not realizing the damage they did. But it was Mother's pain I would carry with me forever, always wishing the path for her had been different.

4.

My trip up north to fetch Mother went smooth as silk. Erika and I had a wonderful afternoon together, shopping and having dinner. The next morning, before picking Mother up for lunch, we attended a yoga class at Erika's gym ("some Zen before the storm," Erika said wryly) and then lunch by the water where Mother seemed in unusually good spirits and accepted the chicken and mushroom sandwich we ordered for her. She slowly sipped a single glass of Chardonnay and, as always, marveled at having two of her three daughters with her. Erika winked.

"That's one."

Stunning us, Mother picked up immediately on the joke.

"I'll say it as many times as I like!" she laughed. Before the afternoon was over, she repeated her astonishment at having two of her three daughters with her at least half a dozen times. Erika and I drove her back to *Menuchat Lev* and I tried to distract Mother while Erika went through the

SHIVAH

mounds and mounds of newspapers and junk mail Mother had collected—a dance that Hannah and Erika concocted once a month and I tried to do whenever I visited—but Mother wasn't buying it. She seemed unusually alert to what we were trying to do. It was easy to see how she had amassed nearly thirty garbage bags of paper that Erika and I had thrown out when we cleaned her house.

Defeated, I lay on the bed next to Mother and told her stories about my life in Virginia and about the temple and about my negotiations last year to get the rabbi a new five-year contract.

"I shouldn't tell you this, though," I said. "You know, you aren't supposed to tell people about the *mitzvot* you do. It sort of negates them."

"How do you know stuff like that?" Mother asked.

Later, at Hannah's, I said that I thought Mother seemed to be doing much better than the past summer.

"She looked well, seemed full of energy. I don't get it."

"It's a weird disease," Hannah said. "She's been much more willing to come here lately, when she wouldn't for months. And I hear from her friends that she goes out with them, does all kinds of things. Beth took her out to lunch and to the theatre last week. But your mother never said a word to me. I look on her calendar and it is full of stuff. But when I ask her, what have you been doing, she says, nothing."

"I know. She tells me you never come see her."

"Oh, Sam, Sam. Did you hear that?"

"Hannah, I heard that."

I said, "She's in the moment. She's washing the dishes."

Hannah looked at me.

"Let me explain," I said.

The next day, I went through Mother's luggage and took out a second pair of slippers, a third pair of black pants and a bathing suit. I made sure I had all of mother's meds, piles of tiny white envelopes marked seven a.m., nine a.m. and bedtime, for each of the four days, plus one day extra, just in case. I realized I had no good idea what was in each of the envelopes: Which were vitamins, which were necessary, which were just for show, if any. But I would give them to Mother diligently, as I did whenever she was in my care.

At the airport, the security guard found Mother's driver's license was expired and he told me that Mother would have to have extra screening. I took him aside quietly and explained that Mother had Alzheimer's: Couldn't something be done? The man went and got his supervisor who said regulations were regulations. I tried to argue with him, and to his credit, he said he would be gentle. I told the man that I must always be with my mother, always in sight of her. He said that would be no problem. But when I explained the situation to Mother, panic flared in her eyes. She grabbed hold of my arm and said, "Don't leave me," over and over. I assured her that I never would.

SHIVAH

After we were through security, I bought Mother a cup of coffee and tried to make a joke of it.

"You really shouldn't wear so much black, Mommy. They obviously thought you were a terrorist."

Mother turned so that her great Romanesque profile was in full view. "It's the nose," she said, laughing.

The rest of the trip went splendidly. Mother insisted on wheeling her own suitcase and walked the airport without complaint, looking glamorous in her long down coat and red cloche, like an aging movie star. The two-hour drive to my house Mother spent looking at the mountains as if she had never seen them before, making only one request: That I find a jazz station on the radio. Once home, I opened the bottle of Mother's preferred cheap Chardonnay and poured her a glass, and while Ivy helped Mother unpack, Paul and I emptied the large bottle down the sink and filled it with a bottle of the non-alcoholic substitute.

For the rest of the time Mother was at the house she poured glass after glass and I didn't have to worry, although I did say, for form's sake, "Slow down, Mom," every once in a while. I thought of the way in which we had tricked her into Sanderstone and the way I was tricking her now. More lies by omission, but what could I do? I tried to find some humor in it. I couldn't help but wonder if Mother knew, but if she was on to me, she said nothing about it. It was then I began to see that the wine was more of a habit, more comfort than an addiction. It was one of the things she remembered doing in her past and it made her feel in control. If Mother was playing along with me, then so be it; in any event, she was far less fuzzy, far easier to engage in conversation, and seemed stronger and more able to manage the time with me and Ivy. She still read the *Providence Journal* she had brought down with her over and over and she continued to read to me, as if it were new every time, the cover story of a month-old *Newsweek*. But she seemed happy to be away from *Menuchat Lev* and neither disoriented nor frightened. She was so much better than she had been more than a year ago at her birthday celebration. There were even tiny moments when she seemed almost, almost, herself.

Erika kept texting me to ask how the visit was going and I kept texting back that it was going fine, until Erika apparently could no longer stand it, could not believe me and texted: *Can you talk?* I called her one evening after Mother had gone to bed.

"It really *is* going well," I said. "Except for the first night when she kept trying to turn on the computers because she thought they were televisions and couldn't understand why there was no reception, there really haven't been any weird moments."

"Wow. That wine substitute thing works, huh?"

"It was your idea."

"I know. Why on earth didn't I ever try it?"

"You will now."

"She doesn't wander around the house getting into things?"

"A little, not so much. Don't forget, my house is much

SHIVAH

smaller than yours and it's all on one floor. That helps.

"And there's more to do here than on the island. We went to Ivy's school. We went for lunch at Sara's, too. Tomorrow we'll go for dinner at the place Ivy works, then to temple. Then it's back home. It worked out fine. We were all worried for nothing."

"If the weather holds."

"If the weather holds."

The weather held. Until it didn't. We got up and made it to the airport in Richmond in plenty of time. The plane was on time. We had already checked it the night before. But then there were delays. And more delays. And then the flight to Boston was cancelled. Mother sat and read her magazine. I remained calm and went to try and change the flight. It turned out we could get on another early the next morning, which meant I would still be able to turn around and be back home the same day. Mother was appalled and kept insisting that she was well enough to fly home alone, but I told her gently that would never do. I insisted to Mother that everything would be all right and that I would prefer, if it was all right with her, to check into a hotel close to the airport rather than turn around and drive two hours back tonight and two in the morning to catch the early flight. Mother threw up her hands and told me I knew what was best.

Once we settled into the Doubletree, I laughed when I saw the pool and remembered chucking Mother's bathing suit out of her suitcase. I also recalled a vacation I had taken with Ben when we were living in France; both of us had neglected to pack suits and had to buy them in a shop in town so that we could use the pool and whirlpool. Since that time I vowed to always pack a suit whenever I traveled and then promptly forgot every time. Now I wished we both had bathing suits and could take a leisurely swim and sit in the hot tub; we had hours to kill.

But Mother had other ideas. She quickly found the lobby bar, climbed up on a stool and ordered a glass of wine. I decided what the hell and ordered a Bloody Mary. We were the only two patrons; it was two o'clock in the afternoon and the waitress kept calling us both sweetie. Mother found that hilarious.

"I can't remember the last time I sat at a bar," Mother said. "Can you?"

I couldn't. We sipped our drinks and ate salted nuts and watched CNBC and commiserated about the stock market and Mother asked me if I was okay financially.

"No," I said, "I'm not. But, then, neither is anyone else I know."

"I'm sorry," Mother said. "I wish I could help."

I looked at her. "I know you do, Mom," I said. "But you have enough to do to take care of yourself."

Then Mother smiled hugely and said, "I am having so much fun, Leah. Thank you. This has been the most wonderful trip. I really thank you for doing this. For taking care of everything. It has been quite an adventure. I can't remember

SHIVAH

the last time I had this much fun."

I almost burst into tears. Instead, I smiled and put my hand over my mother's and said, "You're welcome, Mom. It *has* been fun. I'm glad we did it."

Acknowledgements

I would like to thank Jaded Ibis Press's editors, Elizabeth Earley, Seth Fischer and Vanessa Daunais for acquiring and editing Shivah in a wonderful, collaborative effort that I think has resulted in the best possible version of this novel. Thanks to my early readers, Patti Larimer Young and Donna Shea, and my last reader, my husband Elbert Sholar. I remain eternally appreciative of the more than two decades of fellowships to the Virginia Center for the Creative Arts, a place that nourished me and believed in me before I quite believed in myself, where so very much good writing was done and where I made lifelong friendships with other writers and artists. And finally, I thank my children, Philip and Grace, for making me a mother and, in the process, making me a much better writer. I couldn't have done any of this without you two.